SEX OFFENDERS AND PREVENTIVE DETENTION

SEX OFFENDERS AND PREVENTIVE DETENTION

Politics, Policy and Practice

Bernadette McSherry
BA (Hons), LLB (Hons), LLM (Melb), PhD (York, Canada), Grad Dip Psych (Monash)
Australian Research Council Federation Fellow and Professor of Law, Monash University

Patrick Keyzer
BA (Hons), LLB (Hons), LLM, PhD (Syd)
Professor of Law and Director of the Centre for Law, Governance and Public Policy, Faculty of Law, Bond University

THE FEDERATION PRESS
2009

Published in Sydney by:
The Federation Press
PO Box 45, Annandale, NSW, 2038
71 John St, Leichhardt, NSW, 2040
Ph (02) 9552 2200 Fax (02) 9552 1681
E-mail: info@federationpress.com.au
Website: http://www.federationpress.com.au

National Library of Australia
Cataloguing-in-Publication entry

Sex offenders and preventive detention: politics, policy and practice
Bernadette McSherry and Patrick Keyzer

Includes index.
Bibliography
ISBN: 978186287763 4 (pbk)

Sex offenders - Legal status, laws, etc.
Preventive detention. Criminal Law.

364.153

Typeset by The Federation Press, Leichhardt, NSW.
Printed by Ligare Pty Ltd, Riverwood, NSW.

PEFC™
PEFC/21-31-17

This book has been printed on Australian offset paper certified by the Programme for the Endorsement of Forest Certification (PEFC). PEFC is committed to sustainable forest management through third party forest certification of responsibly managed forests.

Contents

Acknowledgements vii

CHAPTER 1
Three Case Studies 1

CHAPTER 2
The Politics of Risk and Precaution 19

CHAPTER 3
Policy Issues 40

CHAPTER 4
Practical Issues 68

CHAPTER 5
Conclusions 104

References 115

Table of Cases 129

Index 132

Acknowledgements

This book is based on research funded by an Australian Research Council Discovery Project Grant. The authors would like to thank Kathryn Fitzhenry, Tali Budlender and Kathleen Patterson for their invaluable assistance in editing and formatting this book and Sandra Pyke for compiling the Index. Bernadette would like to thank Liz Richardson, Damien Bruckard and Sarah Lenthall and Patrick would like to thank Sian Daniel, Kate Mounsey and Joshua Carson for their research assistance. Thanks also to Christopher Holt and Ann Cunningham at The Federation Press for their support.

CHAPTER 1

Three Case Studies

Introduction

In any society, a small group of convicted offenders may pose a high risk of committing further serious offences. This group presents a significant challenge for governments which must balance the protection of the community with the rights of the offender who has already served time for an offence. In terms of high risk offenders, most of the legislative focus has been on sex offenders, particularly those who commit crimes against children. One response to the management of convicted sex offenders has been to develop preventive detention or supervision schemes which extend governmental control over offenders after the expiry of their prison sentences.

This book focuses on three different legislative models of managing sex offenders: Washington State's approach of detaining 'sexually violent predators' in special institutions, Queensland's post-sentence detention and supervision scheme, and the new Scottish approach of making orders for lifelong restriction at the time of sentence. Our main argument is that legislative regimes which aim *solely* at removing offenders from the community or restricting their movements are resource intensive and may not ultimately succeed in reducing rates of reoffending. In comparing the three models, it is suggested that the Scottish approach is the most appropriate because it is prospective, is closely linked to the offender's crime and treatment is a core component of it. It also has the benefit of being relevant to high risk offenders in general, rather than just sex offenders.

In this chapter, we explore the case studies of three sex offenders who provided the impetus towards the legal enactment of preventive detention and supervision schemes in the three different legal jurisdictions. Earl Shriner, Dennis Ferguson and John Cronin all committed serious sexual offences and the resulting outcry led by the media was fierce and prolonged. Enormous pressure was placed on the respective governments in Washington State, Queensland and Scotland to take action to prevent such crimes recurring.

Because of the outcry by the media and community groups, it is understandable that the governments in these jurisdictions decided to enact laws to detain certain individuals, despite those laws not immediately affecting the three men whose stories are set out here. The case studies are used in this chapter to outline the 'law and order' responses to terrible crimes that captured the attention of the media and the public. What is interesting is that while there was a common political response to enact legislation, the resulting laws were very different. This may be partly explained by the specific circumstances of the events that led to their enactment.

We begin the case studies with the spotlight on Earl Shriner, who grew up in Washington State.

Earl Shriner

In the mid 1960s, at the age of 16, Earl Shriner was labelled a 'defective delinquent' and put into state care. It seems that he had a mild intellectual disability (Boerner, 1991-1992). His mother, Dolores Shriner, described him as having damage 'to the lower lobe of his brain on the left side' (Mooney and Holt, 1989). After he had initially been brought to the attention of the police for choking a seven-year-old girl, Shriner led them to the body of a 15-year-old girl who had been strangled and tied to a tree in the woods (Boerner, 1991-1992). While he was apparently not charged in relation to those crimes, he was detained for some years at the Eastern State Hospital, a regional psychiatric hospital in Washington State.

In 1977, Shriner pleaded guilty to the assault and kidnapping of two 16-year-old girls in Spanaway, Pierce County, Washington. He completed a 10-year sentence for that crime in 1987. Four months after his release, he stabbed a 16-year-old boy in the arm with a knife and served 66 days in the Pierce County Jail for second-degree assault. In December 1988, Shriner was released after serving 67 days for the unlawful imprisonment of a 10-year-old boy whom he had beaten after tying him to a fence post.

At around 9 pm on 20 May 1989, the Mansfield family was burying their family cat in a nearby wood when they saw a young boy, naked, and covered with mud and dried blood. They took him to the hospital where doctors recorded that the seven-year-old boy, Ryan Hade, had been anally and orally raped, stabbed in the back, strangled with a cord and his penis severed. The boy was eventually able to give a description of the man who had attacked him, which matched that of Earl Shriner. Two days after the attack, 39-year-old Shriner was charged with attempted murder in the first degree, rape in the first degree and assault in the first degree.

The assault on Ryan Hade followed soon after the rape and murder of Diane Ballasiotes in Seattle by the released offender Gene Raymond Kane and the combination of these events led to 'a firestorm of community shock and outrage' (Bochnewich, 1992-1993, p 280).

A spokesperson for the then Governor, Booth Gardner, stated that 'there should be a way to involuntarily commit people who have a profile of an individual that is a known risk with a high degree of probability that they would commit this type of crime' (quoted in Boerner, 1991-1992, p 530). Six days after the assault, a group of protesters gathered on the steps of the Capitol Building in Olympia demanding that there be tougher penalties for sex offenders. Diane Ballasiotes' brother, Mike, was a leader of the group. In the week following the assault, 1000 calls and letters were sent to the Governor. This was the most correspondence he had received on a single issue in that space of time (Boerner, 1991-1992, p 534).

Ten days after the assault, 500 people turned up to a public forum on child sexual assault in Tacoma. Some had to view proceedings in an adjacent room on closed circuit television while others were not permitted to enter due to the risk of overcrowding (Glover, 1989).

Ryan Hade spent 10 days at the Mary Bridge Children's Hospital before being allowed home. His mother, Helen Harlow, was quoted as saying 'I think I'll be able to forgive the system when I see that a lifetime of justice is served' (Mooney and Holt, 1989). Nearly $600,000 was donated to a trust fund for the boy (Miletich, 1989).

On 15 June 1989, Governor Booth Gardner set up the Governor's Task Force on Community Protection and asked its members to recommend changes to State law by 1 December of that year. The task force held public hearings throughout Washington State and made a number of recommendations concerning penalties for sex offences as well as the development of a sex offender registry, community notification powers and programs to assist victims. Its most controversial recommendation was for a new civil commitment statute enabling the detention of a small group of sex offenders over whom the State had no existing control.

David Boerner, a legal member of the 24-member task force, stated that the core problem was not the '*exercise* of governmental power but the *absence* of that power' (Boerner, 1991-1992, p 541). That is, the task force had found that there had not been any official negligence or any mistake made in terms of Shriner's release into the community. Rather, there had been no legal power available to detain him. The task force therefore explored a number of possibilities for developing a statutory power to detain. One was the possibility of an indeterminate sentence, but this was thought inappropriate because it could not be applied retrospectively in Shriner's case. Another possibility was to broaden mental health laws to include the detention of sex offenders, but this was dismissed on the basis that it would compromise the basic purpose of the system which was to treat those with mental illnesses.

Instead, the task force decided to explore the avenue of the civil commitment of a specified group of offenders outside of the existing mental health system. Across the United States, legislation had previously existed that enabled States to detain sexual offenders for treatment indefinitely in lieu of sentence. Such laws were often cast broadly to encompass those 'who have committed almost all common sexual offenses [sic] from rape to incest, from indecent exposure to obscene telephoning, from homosexual behaviour to indecent liberties with children, from transvestism to voyeurism' (Di Furia and Mees, 1963, pp 532-533). Because treatment programs for 'sexual psychopaths' under this legislation had been subject to a great deal of criticism, Washington repealed its laws in 1984 (Wash Laws ch 209 1984 codified as Wash Rev Code § 71.06.005 1989) and other States followed suit (Gleb, 1991, p 215).

The task force produced a Bill that enabled post-sentence civil detention for 'sexually violent predators'. This differed from the earlier legislation because it came into force *after* rather than in lieu of sentence. The Bill was enacted as the *Community Protection Act* by the Washington Legislature on 24 January 1990, signed by Governor Gardner on 28 February 1990 and came into effect on 1 July 1990 (Act of 24 January 1990, Wash Laws ch 3, 101-1406 1990).

The *Community Protection Act* and the *Sexual Predator Act* 1990 became known as the Sexually Violent Predator Law (we note changes to the section numbers, which were effected by amendments in 1995,

2003 and 2009, in square brackets below). This law enables the State to detain a person who has served a sentence for a 'sexually violent offense' if it can be shown beyond reasonable doubt that the person 'suffers from a mental abnormality or personality disorder which makes the person likely to engage in predatory acts of sexual violence' (§ 71.09.020(1)). Mental abnormality is defined as 'a congenital or acquired condition affecting the emotional or volitional capacity which predisposes the person to the commission of criminal sexual acts' (§ 71.09.020(2) [§ 71.09.020(8) (2009)]). 'Personality disorder' is not defined.

Once detained, the person is entitled to a new hearing if there is evidence available that the person is unlikely to commit a sexually violent offence (§ 71.09.090 [§ 71.09.090(4)(a-c)]). The person will then be released if the State cannot prove beyond a reasonable doubt that he or she remains a sexual predator (§ 71.09.090(1) [§ 71.09.090(3)(b)]). In the absence of a successful hearing, the person must remain detained until the State determines the person is safe for release (§ 71.09.090(1)). A Special Commitment Center was subsequently built at Monroe to detain and treat those subject to the civil orders.

In May 1989, Earl Shriner pleaded not guilty to rape, assault and attempted murder. When the Pierce County Superior Court judge set bail at $1 million, the spectators in the courtroom cheered (Foster, 1989). On 7 February 1990, after deliberating for six hours, a jury found Shriner guilty of the three charges (Shatzkin and Do, 1990). On 26 March 1990, Judge Thomas Sauriol sentenced Shriner to 131 and a half years in prison, with a non-parole period of 88 years, stating: 'You present a danger to the defenseless' (Carter, 1990). Ironically, the Sexually Violent Predator Law could not apply to Shriner given that it applies to offenders who are at the end rather than at the beginning of their sentence.

Shriner's victim, Ryan Hade, had reconstructive surgery and completed school before enrolling at Bates Technical College to learn upholstery. He left home at 18 and began renovating and selling houses before he died in a motorcycle accident on 9 June 2005, aged 23 (Associated Press, 2005).

Shriner was eventually transferred to the Larned Correctional Mental Health Facility in Kansas, which was built to house offenders in State custody with severe mental illnesses or conduct disorders.

In November 2007, Shriner applied to be transferred to a State hospital for evaluation of his health concerns including what he termed 'a mental block'. This application was dismissed by the Kansas District Court (*Shriner v Rohlings et al*, Civil Action No 07-3306-SAC, 13 February 2008) and an appeal against that decision was also dismissed by the United States Court of Appeals, Tenth Circuit (*Shriner v Rohlings and the State of Washington*, No 08-3048, 17 July 2008).

The case of Earl Shriner set in motion the enactment of sexually violent predator statutes across the United States. The Washington civil commitment provisions were held to be constitutional in a six to three decision by the State Supreme Court on 9 August 1993 (*Re Personal Restraint of Young* 857 P 2d 989 (Wash 1993)), but the Federal District Court in Washington subsequently struck them down (*Young v Weston* 898 F Supp 744 (WD Wash 1995)). Because of these differing viewpoints as to the constitutionality of the civil commitment provisions, Washington State's Attorney-General filed an 'amicus curiae brief' (a brief presented by someone who is not a party to the proceedings, but is interested in the outcome) in relation to similar Kansas legislation which was subject to a constitutional challenge in the United States Supreme Court (Lieb, 1996).

In 1997, the Supreme Court, in a five to four decision, upheld the equivalent Kansas sexually violent predator law as constitutional (*Kansas v Hendricks* 521 US 346 (1997)), giving constitutional approval to previously enacted laws and giving the green light to other States wanting to enact similar legislation. In 2002, the Supreme Court in *Kansas v Crane* 534 US 407 (2002) revisited the *Hendricks* decision, upholding the Kansas law as constitutional, but limiting its application to those having 'serious difficulty in controlling behaviour' (at 870-871). The Supreme Court of the United States has also found the Washington scheme to be constitutional (*Seling v Young* 531 US 250 (2001)). These cases are discussed in more detail in Chapter 3. Eighteen States across the United States have now enacted sexually violent predator laws (New Scientist, 2007a).

Dennis Raymond Ferguson

Dennis Raymond Ferguson was born in 1948. While the circumstances of his upbringing are sketchy, it appears that he was abused as a child (*Ferguson v Watterson* [2008] QDC 224 at [19]).

Ferguson had a long history of convictions for sexual assaults on children. In 1987, Ferguson had a sexual relationship with a 22-year-old fellow prisoner, Alexandria George Brookes, in Long Bay Jail. After they were released, Ferguson befriended a woman whose husband he had met in prison, knowing that her three children had previously been sexually abused. In July 1987, Ferguson and Brookes took the woman's three children, aged six, seven and eight, from their home in Sydney to the Albion Motel in Brisbane. There, the two men sexually abused the children on multiple occasions over a three-day period. Both Ferguson and Brookes were charged with offences against the Queensland *Criminal Code*.

In 1989, Dennis Raymond Ferguson was sentenced to 14 years' imprisonment and Brookes, 11 years. Ferguson's sentencing judge, Justice Des Derrington, described Ferguson's chance of rehabilitation as 'absolutely nil' and stated that Brookes had been led on by Ferguson and was 'somewhat less blameworthy, but not much' (The Courier-Mail, 1988). Ferguson did not participate in any treatment or rehabilitation programs in prison.

Ferguson's impending release from prison on 9 January 2003 gave rise to extensive police and community concerns about the risk that he would reoffend. On the day before he was due to be released, Justice Kenneth Mackenzie of the Supreme Court of Queensland granted an order requiring Ferguson to report to his nearest police station within 48 hours of his release and to advise the police of every plan to change his name and address over the next 15 years (*Director of Public Prosecutions v Ferguson* [2003] QSC 1. Justice Mackenzie stated (p 5) that he was satisfied that 'a substantial risk exists that the offender will commit further offences of a sexual nature upon or in relation to a child under the age of 16'. He based this finding on evidence given by two prisoners of conversations they had with Ferguson. Justice Mackenzie was critical of the way in which the proceedings had been conducted given that Ferguson had been refused Legal Aid and the prisoners' affidavits were only provided at a late stage. He stated (p 4): 'It is important that this situation never happens again'.

Ferguson subsequently moved to New South Wales where he was required under section 9(1) of the *Child Protection (Offenders Registration) Act 2000* (NSW) to give his personal details to the police including the nature of his employment. Ferguson provided the police with these details when first arriving in New South Wales. However, he failed to subsequently notify them of a change of employment. His new job with a cleaning company involved him distributing its products to various places, including schools, for fundraising activities. Ferguson was charged under section 17 of the *Child Protection (Offenders Registration) Act 2000* (NSW) with failing to comply with reporting obligations. The penalty under that section is a $10,000 fine and/or up to two years' imprisonment. In November 2003, Ferguson was sentenced in the Parramatta Local Court to 15 months' imprisonment without parole.

Ferguson was released from prison on 15 December 2004 and initially lived with friends in Brisbane. He then moved to Ipswich to live in temporary accommodation with a friend. In January 2005, Ferguson was the first person to be placed on Queensland's Child Protection Offender Register. The media found out where he was living and 'engendered public support to hound [him] out of town' (*Ferguson v Watterson* [2008] QDC 224 at [2]).

On 1 February 2005, when Ferguson attempted to return to the house from a day out, there was such a crowd of people waiting for him that he had to go to the Yamanto Police Station and be escorted into the house by police. One member of the crowd, Noel Watterson, was later charged and pleaded guilty to making a threat to injure Ferguson.

In relation to Watterson's threat, Ferguson applied for compensation under the *Criminal Offences Victims Act 1995* (Qld). In a hearing in this regard, evidence was presented that Ferguson showed signs of post traumatic stress disorder after being repeatedly bashed and attempts made on his life in prison. A psychiatrist Dr Rosevear stated that the events of 1 February 2005 were 'likely to have added to the burden of morbidity that Mr Ferguson had already suffered up until that time' (*Ferguson v Watterson* [2008] QDC 224 at [19]). District Court Judge Richardson ordered Noel Watterson to pay Ferguson $2250 by way of compensation for the threats.

On 10 November 2005, Ferguson was arrested and charged with the indecent treatment of two children, 'K' and 'B', the offences allegedly occurring on 9 November 2005. On 31 March 2008, a District Court judge ruled there was no evidence to support the charge in relation to 'B' and the Crown Prosecutor entered a nolle prosequi (that is, the Prosecutor made a decision not to go ahead with the prosecution).

The judge suggested that a similar course of action could be taken in relation to 'K', but the Crown Prosecutor decided to proceed. The jury was discharged and a retrial on the charge in relation to 'K' ordered.

A few days before the trial was due to proceed, Ferguson's counsel applied for a stay of proceedings on the basis that pre-trial publicity meant that he could not receive a fair trial and because the Crown's case was very weak. The only evidence directly implicating Ferguson was that of a five-and-a-half-year-old girl who said she was touched by a man, but was not able to identify Ferguson when shown a photoboard containing his photograph along with others. She gave evidence in court that she was touched by Ferguson's 'friend', Allen Guy, who has been convicted of a number of sexual offences involving children.

A stay of proceedings was granted on 1 July 2008. District Court Judge Hugh Botting referred to the evidence as 'tenuous' ([2008] QDC 136 at [25]) and stated that given the pre-trial publicity, it was 'improbable' that a dispassionate jury could be empanelled (at [7]). Ferguson was released from custody (having been on remand since November 2005) and taken to a rural property which he was again forced to leave because of an outcry by residents (Desmond, 2008). When he was relocated to a church property at Carbrook, 600 people turned up to a public meeting at the local school (Munro O'Brien, 2008). The Queensland Police Minister, Judy Spence, stated that there was a 'whole of Government committee working on the next solution for Dennis Ferguson – what we can offer him next' (ABC Stateline Queensland, 2008).

The Attorney-General successfully appealed against the decision to stay the proceedings to the Supreme Court of Queensland (*R v Ferguson; Ex parte Attorney-General (Qld)* [2008] QCA 227). In setting aside the stay, the Court of Appeal stated that it was a matter for the prosecution as to whether to proceed with the charge, and that it was 'hoped that the media will exercise restraint in its reporting of matters relating to [Ferguson]' (at [59]).

Ferguson was placed on conditional bail in relation to the charge against 'K'. His counsel applied for leave to appeal to the High Court from the Court of Appeal's decision, but leave to appeal was refused on 13 February 2009 ([2009] HCA Trans 16). Ferguson was eventually tried before a District Court judge sitting without a jury. Judge Patsy Wolfe acquitted him of the charge against 'K' on 6 March 2009 (The Courier-Mail, 2009). Queensland Police Deputy Commissioner,

Kathy Rynders, was quoted as stating that the police 'will be actively monitoring Mr Ferguson for a period of time ... just as we have done in the months since he was arraigned for trial' (The Courier-Mail, 2009). Ferguson has since moved to Sydney where another public outcry has forced him to move out of his public housing unit (ABC News Online, 2009). This followed the hurried passing of the *Housing Amendment (Registrable Persons) Act 2009* (NSW), which enables the Director-General of the New South Wales Department of Housing to terminate public housing leases of individuals registered under the *Child Protection (Offenders Registration) Act 2000* (NSW).

Ferguson's long history of abusing children has placed him at the forefront of community concerns about paedophiles in Australia and the perceived risks that they pose. Ferguson's case led the Queensland government to enact the *Child Protection (Offender Reporting) Act 2004* (Qld). It also led to the government giving courts the power to make prohibition orders preventing particular sexual offenders from 'engaging in conduct posing a risk to the lives or sexual safety of children' such as loitering near schools or playgrounds (*Child Protection (Offender Prohibition Order) Act 2008* (Qld) s 3).

Most importantly in terms of novel legislative responses, Ferguson's initial release in 2003 provided the impetus for the Queensland government to consider ways of preventively detaining sexual offenders in prison. On 9 January 2003, Queensland's Attorney-General stated: 'Children must and will be protected by our Government ... we're going to make sure that protection of the community, and in particular protection of children, is paramount' (ABC PM, 2003).

In June 2003, the Queensland Parliament enacted the *Dangerous Prisoners (Sexual Offenders) Act 2003* (the 'DPSOA'). It enables the Attorney-General to apply to the Supreme Court for the indefinite detention of a prisoner serving a period of imprisonment for a serious sexual offence. While Ferguson's release was the impetus for this legislation, he of course could not be made subject to it in November 2003 because he was sentenced in New South Wales and for a breach of reporting obligations rather than for a serious sexual offence.

The purposes of the DPSOA are to ensure adequate protection of the community and to provide continuing control, care or treatment of a particular class of prisoners to facilitate their rehabilitation (s 3). The Queensland scheme applies to offenders who are in prison for a serious sexual offence, whether or not the person was sentenced to imprisonment before or after the commencement of the Act. A serious sexual offence is defined as an offence of a sexual nature involving violence or against children (Schedule to the DPSOA). The application period is restricted to the last six months of the prisoner's term of imprisonment 'to ensure that the prisoner is able to take full advantage of any opportunities for rehabilitation offered during the term of imprisonment' (Explanatory Memorandum, Dangerous Prisoners (Sexual Offenders) Bill 2003 (Qld), p 5).

An interdepartmental committee - the Serious Sexual Offenders Review Committee - has been established to refer cases to the Attorney-General for consideration as to whether or not to make an application for preventive detention in a particular case. The Committee comprises senior officers from Queensland Corrective Services, the Department of Justice and Attorney-General and the Queensland Police Service and is chaired by the Deputy Director-General, Correctional Operations.

The Serious Sexual Offenders Review Committee meets monthly to review eligible prisoners and obtain legal advice from Crown Law as to the prospects of success of an application under the Act. The review occurs when the prisoner is 18 months away from full time discharge. The Crown Solicitor makes a recommendation to the Attorney-General who decides whether to proceed with an application. Eligible prisoners are those in custody serving a sentence of more than two years' imprisonment which includes a period for a serious sexual offence. A person who has committed only one offence can be the subject of an order under the DPSOA (*Gadd* [2008] QSC 247).

The first application under the DPSOA concerned Robert John Fardon. On 17 March 1967, Fardon pleaded guilty to the attempted carnal knowledge of a girl under the age of 10 and was sentenced on 17 April 1967 to a good behaviour bond operational for three years. Over the next decade or so, he was convicted of various offences such as theft, drink driving and one count of assault occasioning bodily harm.

On 8 October 1980, Fardon pleaded guilty to rape and indecent dealing with a 12-year-old girl and the wounding of her 15-year-old sister. He served eight years of a 13-year sentence for those offences. Within 20 days of being released on parole, he raped, sodomised and assaulted a woman with whom he had gone to a flat to obtain heroin. On 30 June 1989, he was sentenced to 14 years' imprisonment. There was contradicted evidence that Fardon told a sentence management support officer on 12 March 1998 that he wanted to stay in prison until he died and he would kill an officer or another prisoner to stay there (*Fardon* [2003] QSC 331 at [41]).

Fardon's term of imprisonment was due to expire on 29 June 2003. On 27 June 2003, an interim detention order was granted by Justice Muir who also handed down a ruling on 9 July 2003 that the Act was constitutionally valid (*Fardon* [2003] QSC 200). Fardon appealed to the Queensland Court of Appeal. In *Fardon* [2003] QCA 416, a two to one majority of the Queensland Court of Appeal dismissed the appeal.

Fardon appealed to the High Court of Australia. In October 2004, a majority of the High Court upheld the validity of sections 8 and 13 of the DPSOA, which authorise interim detention orders and continuing detention orders for the preventive detention of serious sex offenders (*Fardon v Attorney-General (Qld)* (2004) 223 CLR 575; Keyzer, Pereira and Southwood, 2004; McSherry, 2005). The appeal was limited to the question whether a power to order further preventive detention of a person in prison was, by authorising a court to imprison a person without a fresh crime and criminal trial, a conferral of jurisdiction upon the Supreme Court of Queensland that was incompatible with its integrity as a court within a constitutional system characterised by a separation of judicial power.

Six of the seven judges (Justice Kirby dissented) held that the Act was valid on the basis that the legislation dealt with a *class* of offenders rather than an individual offender and because sufficient safeguards were in place to ensure the Supreme Court was exercising its judicial discretion in making preventive detention and supervision orders. These constitutional issues are discussed further in Chapter 3. The *Fardon* decision was significant in opening the door for preventive regimes across Australian jurisdictions (McSherry, 2005). The Queensland regime of preventive detention has since been replicated (with some minor differences) in Western Australia and New South Wales with the passing of the *Dangerous Sexual Offenders Act 2006* (WA) and the *Crimes (Serious Sex Offenders) Act 2006* (NSW).

John Cronin

John Cronin was born on 18 July 1971 in Edinburgh. His father, Michael Cronin, was from Limerick and his mother, Jeanette, from East Lothian. John's early years were spent moving between Ireland,

Scotland and the United States. He showed a tendency towards disruptive behaviour from an early age and was reportedly expelled from a private school soon after he was enrolled at age five after he overturned desks, urinated on the floor and attacked teachers (The Scotsman, 2005).

This pattern of behaviour repeated itself in several schools except from the ages of six to eight, when he spent two years at St Margaret's Convent in Edinburgh and his behaviour improved. Cronin eventually obtained four O-grades at a boarding school in Newton Stuart. When he was 17, he received a three-month sentence for indecent exposure and the indecent assault of a 14-year-old classmate. Between 1990 and 1992, Cronin served a number of short prison sentences in Ireland mainly for dishonesty offences.

On 2 May 1992, Cronin went to St Mary's Cathedral in Edinburgh stating that he was a visiting priest, Sean Mulligan, from St Michael's Church in County Cork and was invited to celebrate Mass there. While there he stole a purse, £19 and some papers.

On 21 May 1992, Cronin went to the house of 'Judy X', an Edinburgh Tory party activist and again pretended to be Father Sean Mulligan. After Judy invited him inside, he tried to choke her, punched her, struck her a number of times with a poker, indecently assaulted her and forced her to masturbate him. He then took her jacket and £40 (*Cronin v Her Majesty's Advocate* [1993] SCCR 158).

On 31 July 1992, Cronin pleaded guilty in the High Court at Edinburgh to a number of offences arising out of these events. The unusual circumstances leading up to the assault and the victim's profile meant that there was a great deal of media coverage in the United Kingdom.

At the sentencing hearing, Lord McCluskey had before him reports from Dr Andrew Zealley, a consultant psychiatrist and Director of the Andrew Duncan Clinic at the Royal Edinburgh Hospital, and Dr John Baird, the Physician Superintendent of the State Hospital at Carstairs, Scotland's maximum security hospital.

Dr Zealley suggested that Cronin had a personality disorder and did not recommend any form of therapy. Dr Baird also raised the issue of personality disorder and Cronin's inability to control his behaviour.

On the basis of this evidence, Lord McCluskey stated:

> The picture that emerges … is of a person who is wholly unable to control his behaviour and is suffering from a severe personality

> disorder ... While there was no repeated pattern of violent sexual behaviour in the past, there was really no pattern at all to [Cronin's] behaviour; and he seems to have been engaged since his early childhood in outrageous and uncontrolled behaviour which has become menacing to the public (*Cronin v Her Majesty's Advocate* [1993] SCCR 158).

On the basis of the protection of the public, Lord McCluskey imposed a sentence of life imprisonment.

An appeal was made to the High Court of Justiciary and, on 4 December 1992, that court quashed the sentence of life imprisonment and substituted it with a sentence of six years' imprisonment. Lord Cowie, in delivering the judgment of the Court, stated that life imprisonment is 'an exceptional form of disposal' and was excessive in the circumstances.

Following the lowering of Cronin's sentence, his victim, Judy X, stood up at the Conservative Party Conference and condemned the justice system (BBC News, 2008).

Cronin was released in 1996 and while he has not been charged with any further sexual assaults, he has been in and out of prison for various dishonesty offences and for armed robbery, following an armed raid on a bank in Waterford, Ireland in 2001 (Womersley, 2002). More recently, in September 2007, the Stockholm District Court sentenced Cronin to four months in jail after he ordered a three course meal at an exclusive restaurant and then told waiters he could not pay for it (The Local, 2007). In January 2008, Cronin was jailed for two and a half years after he fraudulently used cheques to pay for expensive hotel rooms and designer clothes (The Scotsman, 2008).

While John Cronin has been categorised by the press as a 'notorious sex offender' (The Scotsman, 2008), his behaviour has been quite different to that of Earl Shriner and Dennis Ferguson. He has been convicted of two indecent assaults, one on a 14-year-old schoolgirl and one on an adult woman, but in the main, his numerous convictions have been for fraud and dishonesty offences.

The MacLean Committee on Serious Violent and Sexual Offenders was established in March 1999 to make proposals for the sentencing, management and treatment of serious sexual and violent offenders who may present a continuing danger to the public. Lord MacLean has been quoted as saying that the Committee's recommendations were influenced by the case of John Cronin (Britten, 2001).

The MacLean Committee presented its report to the Scottish Parliament in June 2000 and public consultation followed. A White Paper (Scottish Executive, 2001) was subsequently prepared which translated the MacLean recommendations into legislative proposals. In a discussion about the White Paper, which took place in the Scottish Parliament on 27 June 2001 (Scottish Parliament, 2001), Roseanna Cunningham, the Scottish National Party member for Perth stated:

> There is no doubt that lifetime restriction orders are needed. The name John Cronin will be well known in the chamber. His case underlines the importance of introducing lifetime supervision for serial sex offenders ... If serial sexual offenders are to be returned to our communities, a mechanism must be put in place to ensure that they are under supervision for as long as they are at liberty.

The history of John Cronin's offending may help explain why the MacLean Committee was not limited to making recommendations for sex offenders alone. The Committee recommended that there should be special sentencing arrangements via orders for lifelong restriction made for a small group of offenders who pose a continuing risk to the public. This enables certain individuals to be under the control of the state for the remainder of their lives, that control initially being of a custodial nature and then under supervision in the community.

The Committee also recommended the formation of a Risk Management Authority which would have a range of responsibilities around assessing risks posed by serious violent and sexual offenders. The system of orders for lifelong restriction and the establishment of the Risk Management Authority were subsequently put in place by the *Criminal Justice (Scotland) Act 2003*. This inserted new provisions into the *Criminal Procedure (Scotland) Act 1995*. The purpose of the Authority is to:

- Develop policy and carry out, commission and monitor research in risk assessment and minimisation.
- Set standards for and issue guidance to those involved in the assessment and minimisation of risk.
- Approve and monitor risk-management plans for those high risk sexual and violent offenders who receive an order for lifelong restriction.

- Accredit people involved in risk assessment and minimisation and the methods and practices used in the assessment and minimisation of risk.
- Carry out education or training activities in relation to the assessment and minimisation of risk (Risk Management Authority, 2009a).

An order for lifelong restriction can only be imposed by the High Court. Before sentencing, once the court determines that certain risk criteria may be met, it is required to make a risk assessment order. The risk assessment order provides for a risk assessor accredited by the Risk Management Authority to carry out a risk assessment and to prepare a risk assessment report. The purpose of the report is to assist the court to make an informed decision about the level of risk an offender poses to the community. If on the basis of this report and other evidence, the court is satisfied on the balance of probabilities that certain risk criteria are met, it must impose an order for lifelong restriction (*Criminal Procedure (Scotland) Act 1995*, s 210F). Such an order is available for those convicted of a single offence but only if the offence is of a serious, violent or life endangering nature and the court is satisfied that the offender meets the statutory risk criteria.

In 2006, Colin Ross became the first person in Scotland to be the subject of an order for lifelong restriction. On 5 July 2006, the 34-year-old Ross attacked a 57-year-old American teacher, Mary Layman-Mendonca, who was visiting Scotland and was walking the last part of the Great Glen Way, which spans 117 kilometres between Fort William and Inverness. Ross beat Layman-Mendonca with an iron bar and a boulder, stole her rucksack and some cash from her shorts, then tied her wrists together with her shoe laces and left her unconscious and bleeding (McFadyen, 2008).

Layman-Mendonca was found by a police officer and she spent three months in a coma in Raigmore Inverness before being moved to hospitals in the United States where she died in late October after having contracted pneumonia.

Previously, in 2003, Ross had been given a two-year sentence for breaching the peace after being found near a woman's home carrying a balaclava and a handwritten note setting out how to carry out attacks on women. After an early release, he was sentenced to three years for attacking a German tourist at Cawdor Castle while wearing a balaclava and gloves (Ross, 2006). After his release in 2006, the police took out a sexual offences protection order against Ross, even though he had no previous convictions for sexual offences, based on the belief that he could be planning further attacks on women (McFadyen, 2008). Six days later, the attack on Layman-Mendonca took place.

Ross had pleaded guilty to attempted murder before the death of Layman-Mendonca. On 18 December 2006, the High Court made an order for lifelong restriction, with a minimum of 20 years to be spent in prison and then, if deemed suitable for release, he would be subject to a risk management plan and supervision for the rest of his life.

Up until June 2008, in the two years following the introduction of the new scheme, a further 17 applications were made to the High Court for orders for lifelong restriction (McFadyen, 2008). Of the eight cases that had been heard during that time, six resulted in an order being made. In the following year, the rate of applications increased considerably and by mid June 2009, 28 offenders had been given orders for lifelong restriction (Risk Management Authority, 2009b).

What is interesting to note about the Scottish approach is that the scheme comes into play at the sentencing stage and depends upon a specifically designed risk assessment process coordinated by a statutory body. The advantages of such an approach will be considered further in Chapter 3.

Conclusion

Over half a century ago, the criminologist Edwin Sutherland (1950, p 142) wrote that 'a community is thrown into panic by a few serious sex crimes, which are given nation-wide publicity; the community acts in an agitated manner, and all sorts of proposals are made; a committee is then appointed to study the facts and to make recommendations'. The reactions to the events described in these three case studies are nothing new. All three cases attracted extensive media coverage and committees were set up in Washington and Scotland to make recommendations for law reform.

What is interesting is that the three jurisdictions differed in their 'solutions' to the management of sex offenders. The Scottish scheme is broadest in scope because it is not restricted to sex offenders, but covers those convicted of serious violent *or* sexual offences, perhaps because John Cronin committed crimes other than sex related ones.

The scheme is brought into play at the time of sentencing, reflecting pre-existing schemes for indefinite detention, but providing a level of treatment and staggered release into the community that is unique.

The Washington and Queensland approaches ventured into new fields for civil commitment laws because of their availability post-sentence. Both schemes were subject to legal challenge, but both have been deemed constitutional. The main differences with the Queensland scheme is that offenders can be detained in prison rather than in specifically designed institutions and offenders can be imprisoned even though they may not be considered to be suffering from a 'mental abnormality'.

The next chapter considers the rise of preventive detention and supervision schemes in light of the politics of risk and precaution. Just because a government may be pressured into passing legislation does not mean that the legislative scheme developed is of necessity unjustifiable or unworkable. On the other hand, legislation enacted with widespread popular support may be ineffective in reducing reoffending. Chapter 3 examines these three schemes from policy perspectives and looks at some of the arguments for and against them.

Chapter 4 will explore some of the practical difficulties that have emerged and the final chapter will make recommendations for law reform in an attempt to balance individual rights with community protection.

CHAPTER 2

The Politics of Risk and Precaution

Introduction

In Philip K Dick's short story 'The Minority Report' (1956), there is a special government branch in New York called 'Precrime', which apprehends those who have been identified by three mutants or 'precogs' as committing murders in the future. While this story is categorised as science fiction, the growing reliance by governments on preventive detention schemes that incarcerate individuals for the purpose of community protection on the basis of what such individuals *might* do is a reality that raises numerous ethical and legal issues.

Criminal justice systems have battled with the perennial issue of what to do with 'dangerous' offenders and their potential for reoffending (McSherry, 2006). In the 19th century, for example, suspected bushrangers could be detained without charge in Australia on the basis of who they were (*Bushranging Act 1830* 2 Geo IV, c 10; Bronitt, 2003). Today, suspected terrorists can be detained without charge on suspicion of future harm (Hogg, 2007; Gani and Mathew, 2008; Zedner, 2009) and there are constant shifts as to which societal groups are subjected to legal control (Pratt, 1998). David Garland (1996, p 461) has explained this historical trend by referring to the concept of the 'alien other' whose dangerousness can only be addressed by removing such individuals from circulation in order to protect the public.

Sex offenders thus form but one 'out' group of society that has captured government, media and public attention (McSherry, 2006). In the words of Jonathan Simon (1998) sex offenders have been constructed as examples of the 'intransigence of evil' and the provisions for preventive detention are thus strategies for 'managing the monstrous'.

As explored in Chapter 1, accounts of sex offenders who have committed sexual assaults after being released from prison have inevitably led to public rage and subsequent legal strategies aimed at preventing future harm. The effectiveness of the legal responses is, however, debatable and often based on questionable assumptions that sex offenders are more dangerous than other offenders and will commit more crimes than any other group. This chapter explores:

- the politics of risk and precaution and why it is that preventive detention schemes have proved politically popular;
- whether sex offenders are indeed more at risk of reoffending than other individuals;
- problems with how risk is assessed by mental health professionals; and
- ethical issues raised by mental health professionals assessing risk for the purpose of detention or imprisonment.

The Politics of Risk and Precaution

There are three main themes identified by criminologists in attempting to explain the political shift toward coercive measures that have developed in order to prevent harm (Ashworth, 2009).

- The first theme refers to the growth of 'actuarial justice' whereby governments encourage 'techniques to identify, classify, and manage groupings sorted by dangerousness' (Feeley and Simon, 1992, p 452; Feeley and Simon, 1994, p 173).
- The second theme focuses on the rise of what has been termed 'the risk society' whereby governments focus on the risks presented by certain individuals or circumstances and act to minimise them (Ericson and Haggerty, 1997; Hudson, 2003).
- The third and most recent theme examines the shift from managing risk towards the necessity to take protective action when the precise nature and scope of potential threats are unknown (Ewald, 2002; O'Malley, 2002; Ericson, 2007; Hebenton and Seddon, 2009).

All of these three themes are relevant to an understanding of why preventive detention and management schemes have developed in relation to sex offenders. The following is an outline of how these themes play out in the political context of policy making.

Lucia Zedner (2007a, p 262) has argued that what marks current criminal justice policy as opposed to that in earlier times, is that neo-liberal societies are 'on the cusp of a shift from a post- to a pre-crime society'. Criminal justice policy has traditionally focused on events post-crime such as the apprehension of offenders, investigation, the trial process and sentencing. Now, however, Zedner argues that there has been a *temporal* shift towards anticipating and stopping what *might* occur in the name of security or community protection.

This theory is borne out by the rise in surveillance techniques, private security companies, offender registers and increasing powers given to police in relation to the investigation, detention and charging of certain individuals such as suspected terrorists *prior* to any crime being committed. There has also been an increase in methods of monitoring certain individuals through the use of orders granted in civil proceedings such as anti-social behaviour orders and terrorism control orders (Zedner, 2007b; Ramsay, 2009).

At the other end of the timeline, the new forms of post-sentence methods of control such as preventive detention and extended supervision orders, primarily for sex offenders, are closely tied in to the desire to prevent future harm. Both pre-crime and post-sentence preventive detention schemes thus stretch the boundaries of the curtailment of liberty beyond the traditional criminal justice approach of state action based on the commission of a crime. Eric Janus (2004a; 2006) refers to this overall trend as that of 'radical prevention' which is characterised by intervention when there is some sort of propensity or risk of future harm and intervention through the curtailment of liberty *before* harm results. Zedner (2006, p 430) points out that preventive measures are advantageous in not having to rely on precise calculations of imminent harm, but bring with them the 'potential to license ever earlier and more intrusive measures' which is 'to say the least, worrisome'.

As well as a temporal shift, Zedner (2007a, p 262) has identified a *sectoral* shift such that the state is no longer the sole instigator of precautionary measures. Instead, there has been a significant increase in the private security industry and more community and territorial means of control. Nikolas Rose (2000a, pp 323-324) has written in this regard:

> There is a widespread recasting of the ideal role of the state, and the argument that national governments should no longer aspire to be the guarantor and ultimate provider of security: instead the state should be a partner, animator and facilitator for a variety of

> independent agents and powers, and should exercise only limited powers of its own …

Rose refers to this trend as governing 'at a distance', such that the criminal justice system has now only a limited role in control practices. Rather, there are broader 'circuits of inclusion' and 'circuits of exclusion' operating in what he terms advanced societies. Circuits of inclusion include all the pieces of information concerning 'our credentials, activities, qualifications for entry into this or that network' (Rose, 2000a, p 325).

Exclusionary strategies are targeted at certain individuals deemed to be beyond the boundaries of 'normal' society. An obvious example of exclusion is the rise of increasing powers of investigation and detention in relation to suspected terrorists as a response to the fear of terrorist attacks (Gani and Mathew, 2008; Zedner, 2009). Similarly, there has been an emphasis on precaution in relation to sex offenders nearing the end of their sentence due to highly publicised incidents of sex offences against children and growing community concerns and fears over safety. The focus is on managing these 'anti-citizens … through measures which seek to neutralize the dangers they pose' (Rose, 2000b, p 195).

These shifts in broadening the scope of preventive and monitoring powers can be viewed as part of an increasing reliance on what has been termed the 'precautionary principle' (Sunstein, 2005; Gardiner, 2006). This principle stems from environmental science and it has been summarised by Carol Raffensberger and Joel Tickner (1999, p 1) as meaning '[i]f there is a potential for harm from an activity and if there is uncertainty about the magnitude of impacts or causality, then anticipatory action should be taken to avoid harm'. Thus, when translated to 'pre-crime' and 'post-sentence' tactics, the precautionary principle ousts evidence-based approaches to public policy (Sunstein, 2005).

The precautionary principle seems to be of particular importance now because of a heightened sense of insecurity in 'neo-liberal' states (Ericson, 2005; 2007). Richard Ericson (2005, p 669) has stated that the 'criminalization of uncertainty' is currently the preferred response in the 'face of limited knowledge about threats'.

In the context of precautionary politics, it is understandable that governments have viewed the management of sex offenders as being of crucial community concern (Hebenton and Seddon, 2009). In the words of Eric Janus (2004a, p 592), the risk that certain offenders pose to the community 'quietly takes the place of race, gender, sexual orientation and disability in the outsider jurisprudence'. How risk is assessed and the problems posed by risk assessment methods are discussed later in this chapter. What is important to understand is that the rise of preventive detention and supervision schemes for sex offenders is part of 'the wider politics of fear and insecurity' (Seddon, 2008, p 312) and the emphasis on risk assessment in relation to sex offenders adopts 'a technology of categorical exclusion' (O'Malley, 2002, p 211).

The trend towards preventive detention is generally based on the assumption that sex offenders are at the highest risk of reoffending and therefore precautionary measures are justifiable. The next section analyses whether this is in fact the case.

Sex Offenders and the Risks Posed by Them

The label 'sex offender' encompasses individuals who have committed a wide range of offences, from exhibitionism to opportunistic rape or child abuse to numerous assaults on family members over a long period of time to a one-off offence amongst a long train of diverse crimes. However, preventive detention schemes usually make little distinction between sub-categories of sex offenders (Demleitner, 2003, p 1627).

The 'archetypal' sex offender of the public's imagination is that of the paedophile preying on young children, an image which causes reactions exemplified by those outlined in Chapter 1 concerning Earl Shriner and Dennis Ferguson. Sometimes, the word 'sex offender' will also conjure up the image of a violent rapist of adult women as personified by the reactions to John Cronin's sex offence.

However, the sex offender of popular imagination, the predator who persistently targets vulnerable strangers, particularly children, is rare (Lievore, 2005). There is a growing body of evidence that most sex offenders know their victims, most do not have a psychiatric illness and most are never convicted for their crimes (Gelb, 2007). In fact, it appears that most sexual offending is carried out 'by men connected to their victims as family or friends, operating under a façade of "normal" relationships' (Gelb, 2007, p 10).

In addition, most serious violent criminals do not have previous convictions for violence and do not repeat their violent offending (Walker, 1996, pp 7-8). There is a small group of high risk offenders who do pose a risk of committing further serious violent or sexual offences. Yet, it must be kept in mind that 'members of the public face a greater likelihood of suffering violent crime at the hands of people who consume too much alcohol or illegal drugs, than as a result of the actions of any identifiable and separate group of high risk offenders with a propensity for acting violently' (Committee on Serious Violent and Sexual Offenders, 2000, p 5).

The central issue for any preventive detention and management scheme is to identify exactly who presents a high risk of committing further serious offences. There is an assumption that sex offenders are at a higher risk of reoffending than other offenders, but this may not necessarily be the case.

One study has concluded that there is no empirical evidence supporting the conclusion that sex offenders are more likely to engage in repeat offending than non-sex offenders (Simon, 1997). Another concluded that sex offender recidivism (reoffending) and rates for revoking parole for sex offenders are lower than for other offenders on parole (Sample and Bray, 2003). One review (or 'meta-analysis') of studies examining recidivism rates of sex offenders, while acknowledging problems of relying on reconviction rates and the limited follow-up periods of some studies, indicated that only 13.4 per cent of convicted sex offenders committed a new sexual offence within four to five years (Hanson and Bussière, 1998). Similarly, in a review of 95 studies that had a combined sample of over 31,000 sexual offenders, R Karl Hanson and Kelly Morton-Bourgon (2004) estimated the rate of sexual recidivism to be 13.7 per cent after approximately five years. This is much lower than for other types of offending including other violent crimes (Sullivan, Mullen and Pathé, 2005, p 319).

There are of course problems with estimating rates of reoffending for sex offenders given that many sexual offences remain undetected or unreported, but the available research does not support the premise that sex offenders inevitably reoffend or that they are more likely to reoffend than other groups of offenders.

Despite the growing literature debunking some of the myths about sex offenders, recent legislative responses 'appear to hinge on the false assumptions that previously convicted sex offenders pose the main threat, and that imposing severe penalties on them will solve the problem' (New Scientist, 2007b). This may have the unwanted consequence of placing the majority of resources into managing a small group of sex offenders to the detriment of measures that could target the majority of sex offenders, most of whom are not charged and who go untreated (Chung, O'Leary and Hand, 2006; Miethe, Olson and Mitchell, 2006).

The Role of Mental Health Professionals in Assessing Risk

All three approaches to the management of sex offenders discussed in this book rely on assessments of risk and all three require the input of mental health professionals. Usually a decision concerning preventive detention or supervision will require the evidence of at least one psychiatrist. In general, psychiatrists have a medical degree, which involves six years of studying general medicine, followed by further study to specialise in psychiatry. Evidence may also be given by psychologists who study human behaviour in their undergraduate and postgraduate degrees before undertaking supervised experience and gaining registration, but who do not have a medical degree. In Scotland, there is also a general acceptance of reports by social workers throughout the criminal justice system (Expert Panel on Sex Offending, 2001, p 25).

Under the *Dangerous Prisoners (Sexual Offenders) Act 2003* (Qld), two psychiatrists are required to examine the individual concerned (s 9) and provide a report which includes a statement concerning the level of risk that the individual will commit another serious sexual offence (s 11(2)). The court must decide whether the individual is a 'serious danger to the community' based on whether there is an 'unacceptable risk' that the individual will commit a serious sexual offence if released (s 13(2)). In reaching this decision, the court must have regard to the psychiatric material and any other reports including those by psychologists and other health professionals (s 14).

In Washington, under the *Community Protection Act 1990*, a judge first determines whether 'probable cause exists' to believe that the individual is a 'sexually violent predator' (§ 71.09.040(1)) and if so, orders that the individual is transferred to an 'appropriate facility' for an evaluation (§ 71.09.040(4)). It is up to the Department of Social and Health Services to establish rules as to who can conduct the evaluation

(§ 71.09.040(4)), but in practice this will usually be a psychiatrist or psychologist (Special Commitment Center, 2009). The individual concerned also has the right to be examined by a 'qualified expert or professional person of his or her own choice' (§ 71.09.050(2)).

At the hearing, it must be proved beyond reasonable doubt that the person is a sexually violent predator (§ 71.09.060(1)). This requires consideration of whether the person 'suffers from a mental abnormality or personality disorder which makes the person likely to engage in predatory acts of sexual violence if not confined in a secure facility' (§ 71.09.020(16)). Such a likelihood is further defined as meaning that the individual 'more probably than not' will engage in such acts if released unconditionally from detention (§ 71.09.020(7)). The Washington State legislation has served as a model for other State-based sexually violent predator legislation and thus similar requirements apply in relation to other civil preventive detention schemes in the United States.

In Scotland, under the *Criminal Procedure (Scotland) Act 1995*, the High Court may make a risk assessment order so that the offender can be assessed by a person accredited by the Risk Management Authority (s 210B). Assessors must have a professional background and are usually psychiatrists or psychologists, but other professionals such as social workers can also apply for accreditation.

The assessor prepares a risk assessment report which must state the risk of reoffending as high, medium or low (s 210C(3)). In making an order for lifelong restriction, the High Court must have regard to the risk assessment report and any other relevant reports in order to assess whether, on the balance of probabilities, the risk criteria have been established (s 210F). The Scottish risk criteria (s 210E) include considering whether there is 'a likelihood' that the offender, if at liberty, will seriously endanger the lives, or physical or psychological well-being of members of the public at large.

All three schemes thus require relevant mental health professionals to give evidence as to the likelihood that the individual concerned will harm others in the future. Identifying which individuals are at risk of future offending involves predicting future human behaviour and the reliance on the expertise of mental health professionals in this regard is a relatively recent phenomenon.

Since the 19th century, medical experts have been called upon to give their expert opinions in courtrooms in relation to the mental states of certain individuals (Eigen, 1995; Gutheil, 2005). However, requiring evidence as to whether a particular individual is at risk of reoffending has its origins alongside the rise of the politics of risk. As Simon (1998, p 453) points out, the role of risk assessment has 'become more formal and associated with statistical forms of inference'.

Assessing the risk of future violence is a notoriously difficult task (Mullen, 2001; Johnson, 2005) and while the state of knowledge on risk assessment has improved in recent years, no current assessment procedure can predict risk with certainty.

During the early 1980s, research suggested that mental health professionals tended to be especially cautious in their assessments of possible future offending and to over-predict violence (McAuley, 1993, p 7). One study concluded that these predictions were accurate in only about one third of cases (Monahan, 1981). Such over-prediction has been shown to result in large numbers of 'false positives', where individuals have been identified as likely to commit further offences but who, upon release, have not actually reoffended (Steadman, 2000). During this time, the emphasis was on making clinical assessments of 'dangerousness', which did not provide a medical diagnosis, but involved 'issues of legal judgment and definition, as well as issues of social policy' (Steadman, 2000, p 266).

Between the mid 1980s and the mid to late 1990s, the focus shifted from assessing dangerousness to a focus on assessment scales based on statistical or actuarial risk prediction. These scales assess the particular offender against a range of factors that are known to be associated with future offending (Rose, 1998; Berlin, Galbreath, Geary and McGlone, 2003). This shift to risk assessment and risk management has seen the rise of 'scientific' literature examining a range of risk factors that have a statistical association to a future event.

A range of actuarial risk assessment scales is now used particularly in North America and the United Kingdom to measure the risk of reoffending. Instruments such as the Psychopathy Check-List Revised (PCL-R) (Hare, 1991), the Violence Risk Appraisal Guide (VRAG) (Quinsey, Harris, Rice and Cormier, 1998) and the Historical/Clinical/Risk-20 (HCR-20) (Webster, Douglas, Eaves and Hart, 1997) focus on variables that are said to have been ascertained by actuarial studies (Norko and Baranoski, 2005). The Macarthur Study of Mental Disorder and Violence has also led to the development of a classification tree model referred to as an 'iterative' classification tree (ICT) (Monahan, Steadman, Silver et al, 2001).

Paul Mullen (2001) outlines how assessments of risk deal in general with the following issues:

- **past violence** (on the assumption that the best predictor of future violence is past violence);
- **pre-existing vulnerabilities** (such as being male, anti-social traits, suspiciousness, childhood marred by disorganisation and/or abuse, youth, impulsivity and irritability);
- **social and interpersonal factors** (such as poor social networks, lack of education and work skills, itinerant lifestyle, poverty and homelessness);
- **symptoms of mental illness** (such as active symptoms, poor compliance with medication and treatment, poor engagement with treatment services, treatment resistance and lack of insight into the illness);
- **substance abuse** (particularly alcohol abuse);
- **state of mind** (such as the presence of anger or fear, delusions that evoke fear or provoke indignation or produce jealousy, clouding of consciousness or confusion, ideas of influence, and command hallucinations);
- **situational triggers** (such as loss, demands and expectations, confrontations, ready availability of weapons, and physical illness); and
- **personality constructs** (such as psychopathy).

The last category of personality constructs is perhaps the most controversial of predictor variables for violence. Hare (2002, p 27) states that psychopathy is 'a personality disorder defined by a cluster of interpersonal, affective, and lifestyle characteristics that results in serious, negative consequences for society. Among the most devastating features of the disorder are a callous disregard for the rights of others and a propensity for predatory behaviour and violence'.

The assessment scale called the Psychopathy Checklist-Revised (PCL-R) has been hailed as the 'unparalleled' single predictor of violence (Salekin et al, 1996). However, its use as a predictive tool can still be questioned (Cooke and Michie, 2009) and the terms 'psychopath' and 'antisocial personality disorder' have been criticised as being social constructs (Cavadino, 1998; McCallum, 2001). John Ellard (1996, p 62) points out:

> If you are a rather disagreeable small-time thief with a bad temper you are likely to be described as suffering from Antisocial Personality Disorder. If without any contrition you waste millions of dollars of other people's money and achieve nothing but notoriety you will be called an entrepreneur.

The debate as to the limitations of personality constructs as a predictor of future violence continues (Cooke and Michie, 2009).

In relation to sex offenders, the Static-99 (Hanson and Thornton, 1999), the Sex Offender Need Assessment Rating, generally referred to as SONAR (Hanson and Harris, 2000) and the Sexual Violence Risk-20 (SVR-20) (Boer, Hart, Kropp and Webster, 1997) are sometimes used. Like the more general actuarial-based scales, they include questions dealing with a number of variables. The Static-99 is intended to be used on adult sex offenders and consists of 10 items dealing with static variables such as age, persistence of sexual offending, 'deviant' sexual interests, relationship to victims and general criminality. The SONAR aims to measure changes in risk factors by measuring dynamic factors such as non-cooperation with supervision, access to victim(s), sexual pre-occupations, anger and acute changes in mood. The SVR-20 consists of 20 items dealing with the offender's 'psychosocial adjustment', history of sexual offending and future plans. In 2003, the Risk of Sexual Violence Protocol (RSVP) (Hart et al, 2003) was developed to build on the SVR-20 while revising some items and adding more.

All of these scales are based on variables that apply across individuals and give rise to the 'statistical truism that the mean of a distribution tells us about everyone, yet no one' (Cooke and Michie, 2009). Applying knowledge of group tendencies to individual offenders may have dire consequences when transferred to court settings. As well as criticisms of the reliability of individual actuarial scales (Ward and Eccleston, 2000), there have been a number of problems identified with the *use* of actuarial-based scales in relation to individual offenders. Some of these criticisms include:

(1) Static/Historical Variables

Risk assessment scales largely focus on variables that are historical in nature (Sullivan, Mullen and Pathé, 2005, p 319). The main focus is on static risk factors that cannot change over time, such as the age of first offending and childhood abuse. Risk assessment scales do not consider current clinical variables (such as response to treatment or motivation), moderating factors (such as stable employment) or variables that reduce the risk of reoffending (such as physical illness or frailty). Hanson has argued that there is a need to include dynamic variables as well - ones that can change over time, such as coping strategies - to ensure risk assessments become more accurate and in order to identify useful treatment (Hanson, 2002; see also Hanson, Harris, Scott and Helmus, 2007).

There is some evidence of awareness of the limitations of the static tests in the case law (*McLean* [2006] QSC 137; *Tillman* [2007] NSWSC 605 at [72]-[76] per Bell J (as her Honour then was); *Gadd* [2008] QSC 247). But in many cases the use of static tests passes without judicial comment on their potential unreliability (see for example, *Carpenter* [2008] QSC 225 at [28]; *RJE* [2008] VSCA 265 at [93] per Weinberg JA). Research into the effect of dynamic factors on the risk of reoffending is in its infancy and there is little to guide assessors in relation to determining whether offenders have benefited or changed as a result of treatment (Mercado and Ogloff, 2006, p 55).

(2) Applying Group Data to the Individual

Actuarial scales are based on determining whether an individual offender has the same characteristics or risk factors as a 'typical' kind of offender (Campbell, 2000; 2003). Risk assessments can classify an individual within a group - as 'high risk', 'medium risk' or 'low risk' - but they cannot say where in this group a given person lies and therefore cannot identify the precise risk an individual poses. Assigning risk to an individual offender based on the characteristics of a group can therefore lead to inaccurate assessments (Janus and Prentky, 2003) which in turn raises issues for expert testimony concerning individuals (Cooke and Michie, 2009). In the words of John Petrila (2004, p 10):

> In some circumstances [in legal proceedings], clinicians have not acknowledged the limitations of the instruments, leading to situations in which courts have characterized the instruments as able to 'predict' future sexual offending in individual cases; this has the practical effect of inappropriately transforming a tool for assessing probabilities for future offending into something perceived as predictive for the defendant before the court.

(3) Differences in Particular Groups

Actuarial risk assessment scales may also pose difficulties when used with particular groups of offenders. For example, Indigenous offenders as a group have higher rates of childhood abuse victimisation and early substance abuse, both of which are included in the assessment questionnaires as factors associated with high risk status. Indigenous offenders may therefore be more likely to be classified as high risk than are non-Indigenous offenders (Sullivan, Mullen and Pathé, 2005, p 319). Expert witnesses and at least one judge in Australian cases have questioned whether instruments that have not been validated through studies involving Australian Indigenous offenders should be relied on in Australian courts (*McLean* [2006] QSC 137 at [26]; *George* [2009] QSC 2 at [33]; *Mangolamara* [2007] WASC 71 at [165]-[166]).

(4) Translating Predictions for Treatment to the Courtroom

The use of risk assessment scales may be justifiable for the purpose of treatment in a clinical environment, but problems with such scales are amplified by their use in legal forums, where they can be 'prone to manipulation and misinterpretation' (Sullivan, Mullen and Pathé, 2005, p 319). They can lead to unnecessary detention due to 'false positives'.

On the basis of such criticisms, Frank Farnham and David James (2001, p 1926) have questioned the whole premise that such scales are scientific in nature:

> Would-be clairvoyants engaged in this form of assessment exercise will make use of 'tools' in the form of actuarially-based checklists, which give spurious scientific value to estimations that perform less well than chance.

Because of the criticisms of actuarial risk assessment scales, some mental health professionals have called for a combination of actuarial and clinical methods of assessment in order to produce better results tailored to the individual (Hanson, 2003, p 67). The process of combining clinical and actuarial approaches has been termed 'structured assessment' (Heilbrun, Ogloff and Picarello, 1999) or 'structured clinical judgment' (Report of the Committee on Serious Violent and Sexual Offenders, 2000).

There is tension amongst some mental health professionals as to which professionals are best suited to carry out risk assessments.

Cynthia Mercado and James Ogloff (2006, p 57), two forensic psychologists, have criticised the Queensland scheme for requiring two assessments from psychiatrists on the basis that there is no evidence that 'psychiatrists are any better able to predict risk for violence or sexual offending than psychologists'. They point out (2006, p 58) that the majority of research published on risk assessment has been conducted by psychologists.

On the other hand, some psychiatrists have been at the forefront of criticisms of the over-reliance on actuarial scales, emphasising the importance of clinical judgment and diagnostic abilities based on medical training. The Royal College of Psychiatrists for the United Kingdom and the Republic of Ireland (2005, p 75) has pointed out:

> There appears to be a consensus view among British forensic psychiatrists that clinical assessment has an ethically justifiable edge over other risk measures because they are individually sensitive and dynamic. Actuarial risk measures should therefore be presented in the context of clinical assessment.

Overall, while risk assessment techniques have advanced over the past decades, Herschel Prins' (1996) view that there is no ideal, or even sophisticated, approach available to the assessment of risk remains of concern. In the words of Andrew Carroll, Mark Lyall and Andrew Forrester (2004, p 413), '[n]o method, clinical, actuarial or combined, achieves anywhere near 100% predictive power, whether short or long term risk is considered'. It would seem that risk assessment should vary according to the characteristics of the individual, situation and potential victim along with the number of cumulative risk factors experienced by the offender. The use of risk assessment scales and clinical judgment may be justified in clinical environments, but another level of criticism overlays the use of assessments in the legal system. We now turn to the ethics of giving such evidence in the courtroom and the issues posed by such evidence informing preventive detention schemes.

The Ethics of Risk Assessment and the Courts

While mental health professionals who give evidence in court about offenders' risk of reoffending are often cross-examined, there is some question about whether such evidence should be admitted at all (Ruschena, 2003). These assessments of risk tend to be taken out of their primary context, which is one of treatment and intervention (Ruschena, 2003, pp 127-128). There is also the potential for judges and juries to misunderstand and misuse risk assessments, assigning greater accuracy and inevitability to predicted behaviours than is warranted (Johnson, 2005). In addition there are issues as to what level of risk (low/medium/high) should be required by such schemes and to what level of offending the risk should relate (any offending/serious offending/serious 'relevant' offending).

Asking mental health professionals to assess the risk of future harm shifts the burden of deciding what to do with such offenders from the community to clinicians whose primary role lies within the medical model of treatment, rather than within the criminal justice model of punishment and community protection. This in turn raises questions about the ethics of mental health professionals giving evidence that may lead to the deprivation of liberty *after* offenders have served their time. The following section outlines some of the arguments that have been made in this regard.

Argument 1: It is Always Unethical to Give Testimony on Risk

The dual role of mental health professionals in providing treatment as well as opinions for court purposes is a vexed one. More than two decades ago, Alan Stone (1984) started a debate in the United States about the ethics of forensic psychiatry, arguing that as a matter of individual ethical commitment, he could not justify himself giving evidence for the purposes of the criminal justice system. While he did not go so far as to say that psychiatrists should *never* testify in court, he pointed out that those who did so risked violating the ethics relevant to those whose primary duty was to treat individuals.

Three years later, Gary Melton, John Petrila, Norman Poythress and Christopher Slobogin (1987, p 204) argued that, in relation to risk assessment, there is 'no specialized clinical knowledge that permits categorical, or even relative conclusions about dangerousness'. As a result, they stated (p 205) that mental health professionals 'may decide that they cannot ethically offer prediction testimony'. More adamantly, Charles Ewing (1991, p 162) has argued that '[t]he psychiatrist or psychologist who makes a prediction of dangerousness violates his or her ethical obligation to register judgments that rest on a scientific basis'. Similarly, Eric Janus (2004b, p 50) has stated that the indeterminacy of legal terms such as 'likely' or 'highly likely' require mental health professionals to 'make political judgments that determine the balance between public safety and individual liberty'.

The Royal College of Psychiatrists for the United Kingdom and the Republic of Ireland held a seminar on the ethics of giving evidence for extended sentencing purposes in 2002. It published an overview of the discussion in the *Psychiatric Bulletin* in 2005 and stated that one view aired was that 'it is not ethically part of medicine to assist the courts in increasing punishment and public protection by applying medical skills to such a purpose' (Royal College of Psychiatrists, 2005, p 75).

Refusing to engage in risk assessments for the purposes of the criminal justice system on the basis that it is unethical to do so is obviously an extreme action. Risk assessment not only informs decisions concerning the detention of offenders, but also the law relating to the civil commitment of individuals with mental illnesses, and child protection. In reality, only a few mental health professionals will take this extreme approach, but such a position does force mental health professionals to consider whether and in what circumstances giving such testimony is justifiable.

Argument 2: It is Always Ethical to Give Testimony on Risk

At the other end of the scale to refusing to engage in assessing risk for the courts is the argument that mental health professionals must always perform their job and leave any ethical justifications to other professionals. Thomas Grisso and Paul Appelbaum (1992, p 630) have outlined this position as being one that leaves 'questions of justification to the courts and society to determine, not the mental health professionals'. Thus it is for Parliament to create laws restricting the liberties of individuals and for mental health professionals to comply with what is legally required of them in this regard.

The main problem with this approach is that it makes mental health professionals agents of state control, which can have dire consequences for certain groups of individuals. One extreme example of this occurred during the Nazi era when psychiatrists were 'instrumental in instituting a system of identifying, notifying, transporting, and killing hundreds of thousands of mentally ill and "racially and cognitively compromised" individuals in settings ranging from centralized psychiatric hospitals to prisons and death camps' (Strous, 2007; see also Seeman, 2005). It also ignores the obligations placed on mental health professionals through various codes of ethics to comply with ethical standards and even to seek changes in laws when they are contrary to the best interests of individuals (for example American Psychiatric Association, 2009, s 3).

There is a body of literature predominantly on psychiatric ethics which attempts to steer a path through these two extremes.

Argument 3: It is Ethical to give Testimony on Risk in Certain Circumstances

The Royal College (2005, p 75) has outlined a number of approaches that attempt to find a mid-way point between the extremes of refusing to engage in risk assessments and always engaging when required by legislation.

One approach is to extend acting for the benefit of the patient under traditional medical ethics to acting for the benefit of the offender. That is, forensic psychiatrists should assume when accepting a call for risk assessment by the courts that there is always some prospect of treatment or benefit available to the offender concerned. This may be a less than ideal approach, however, when it is known that there is inadequate treatment available as part of preventive detention schemes. This issue is explored in Chapter 4.

Another approach to extending existing medical ethics is to act only where it is known that the offender will indeed receive some form of individual health benefit. Going one step further, this could mean acting only on behalf of the offender rather than for the state. This however assumes that mental health professionals will know when treatment is available and when it will be of benefit. It may also lead to a refusal to assess certain individuals who are not considered 'treatable', thus depriving them of any form of expert evidence.

A more practical approach is to use a different ethical framework for forensic testimony beyond that of medical ethics which attaches such importance to treatment. The Royal College refers to this as 'justice ethics', which appears to stem from Paul Appelbaum's view (1984; 1990; 1997a) that forensic psychiatry should use a framework of ethics based on 'truth' rather than 'beneficence'. This approach requires the fundamental value of truth telling and respect for the individual, with the ultimate goal being to advance justice rather than to act for the benefit of the individual patient. The principle of truth telling requires testifying as to what the mental health professional believes to be true, regardless of whether this advantages or disadvantages the particular offender, but it also requires an accurate presentation of the scientific data available and the consensus of the field (Appelbaum, 2008). In relation to testimony using actuarial scales, for example, this principle would require the mental health professional to outline the limitations of the scales used (Morse, 2008).

The principle of respect for persons requires respect for the individual being assessed. In Appelbaum's words (2008, p 197), this requires that mental health professionals should not 'engage in deception, exploitation, or needless invasion of the privacy of the people who we examine or about whom we testify'.

In relation to risk assessment, Thomas Grisso and Paul Appelbaum (1992, p 631) have argued that a mid-way point is to see predictive testimony as neither ethical or unethical in itself, but the *use* of the testimony may be ethical or unethical given the variability in the types of liberty restrictions involved. This leads on to the final argument.

Argument 4: It is Ethical to Give Testimony on Risk in Certain Circumstances, but not for Post-sentence Preventive Detention Schemes

A slightly different version of the third argument is to view the giving of risk assessment testimony as unethical in the situation where the legal consequences of the prediction lead to a loss of liberty outside of the criminal justice system. On this basis a distinction can be drawn between the ethics of risk assessment at the time of sentence and at the time when the sentence has concluded.

Danny Sullivan, Paul Mullen and Michele Pathé are three psychiatrists working in Victoria who have questioned the ethics of requiring clinicians to assess risk for the purposes of continued coercive supervision after sentence. They have pointed out that being required to give evidence for preventive detention schemes raises the spectre of mental health professionals being 'agents of supervision, social control and monitoring' rather than 'independent clinicians' (2005, p 320).

The Royal College (2005, p 75) noted that there 'may be an ethical argument for ensuring that disagreements regarding mental disorder and risk are considered early on at the point of sentencing when the court, rather than doctors, can decide these issues'.

This position may run into the same problem in reality as that in relation to a complete refusal to engage in providing testimony for the criminal justice system - there will always be some mental health professionals willing to engage with legislative requirements to provide assessments of risk for post-sentence preventive detention. However, at the very least, this position does raise the issue of mental health professionals being agents of social control and provides a starting point for distinguishing between the justifications for risk assessment for sentencing purposes within the criminal justice system as opposed to risk assessment for 'civil' forms of detention outside of the criminal justice system.

Conclusion

There has been a long tradition of laws targeting 'out' groups in society. The current trend towards precautionary measures differs from past attempts to curtail individual liberty because of the broadened scope of 'pre-crime' measures and because of the focus of detention on the basis of future rather than past or attempted harm.

Preventive detention and supervision schemes in Queensland, Scotland and Washington all require evidence to be given by mental health professionals before a court can make an order. The structured approach to risk assessment (Heilbrun, Ogloff and Picarello, 1999) which combines both actuarial scales and clinical judgment is a more sophisticated approach than clinical judgment alone, but it is nowhere near perfect. Cynthia Mercado and James Ogloff (2006, p 57) have stated that despite advances in risk assessment techniques, the role of mental health professionals 'in any preventive detention schemes must be necessarily limited'. They emphasise that it is up to 'legal decision makers' to make the call as to whether an offender meets the criteria for preventive detention. A similar approach has been taken by Stephen Morse (2008) in arguing that the role of the forensic psychiatrist should be limited to helping legal decision makers evaluate mental states and that they should steer clear of the 'ultimate issue' - whether it be if an offender was mentally ill at the time of the crime or is at risk of future offending.

Early this century, psychiatrists and other individuals involved in the mental health system in England staged a concerted attack on the government's proposal to allow the involuntary hospitalisation of 'dangerous people with severe personality disorders' solely for the purpose of managing problematic behaviour rather than for the purpose of treatment or because they had committed a crime (Seddon, 2007; 2008). More than 50 organisations, including the Royal College, formed the Mental Health Alliance to lobby against the proposed legislation (Appelbaum, 2005) and many editions of the *British Medical Journal* and the *Psychiatric Bulletin* contained articles and letters condemning the proposal (see for example Mullen, 1999; Haddock et al, 2001; Birmingham 2002; Coid and Maden, 2003). Some critics of the proposal raised similar ethical questions about being agents of social control (Corbett and Westwood, 2005). This concerted opposition to the proposal at least forced the government to rethink its approach and to redraft its proposed legislation (Hebenton and Seddon, 2009), although Dangerous and Severe Personality Disorder programs and services have been established (DSPD Program) and have ironically been praised for providing effective mental health services to a group of offenders in dire need of such services (Mullen, 2007).

While criticisms of preventive detention schemes have been apparent in the United States and Australia, the speed at which the Australian and United States schemes have been passed has given little time for consultation or dissent that could give rise to policy reform. The precautionary principle leads to a 'precautionary mentality within government that says "do something quickly" rather than adopt a more cautious, deliberative approach to change' (Goldsmith, 2008, p 160). There may also be differences concerning the impetus for lobbying governments, given that in the United Kingdom the vast majority of forensic psychiatrists are employed within the National Health Service by publicly funded mental health services, whereas the converse may be more usual in the United States (Grounds, 2005).

Despite the absence of concerted lobbying *prior* to the introduction of preventive detention schemes in the United States and Australia, it appears that psychiatrists in particular are discomforted by the reliance on risk assessment in the courts. Henry Steadman (1972-1973, p 270) pointed out some decades ago that '[f]orensic psychiatry is intimately connected with the political forces of social control. Its legitimation appears to be greatly tied up in its ability to apply social control in a manner favorable to existing power structures'. More recently, Michael Robertson and Garry Walter (2008, p 234) have stated that 'the ethical quandaries of psychiatry, and the values psychiatrists bring to these, integrate social and cultural issues as much as clinical ones'. Forensic psychologists have generally concentrated more on evaluating and criticising risk assessment tools rather than engaging with critically evaluating their use in the courtroom. This may be because 'psychology in general focuses on researching the human psyche (especially its cognitive components) and does not deal easily with issues of a sociopolitical nature' (Bar-On, 2001, p 333).

Many mental health professionals will continue to be willing to provide evidence of future risk as required by preventive detention schemes, but the ethics of doing so remains of concern.

The 'objectification' of risk through structured clinical judgment disguises a moral condemnation of certain groups in society. Predictions of risk can be viewed as providing a veil of science over what is essentially a social and moral decision about the kind of offender who creates the greatest fear within the community. In the words of Barbara Hudson (2003, p 67):

> The morally neutral scientific, actuarial terminology of risk disguises the condemnatory pariahdom created by the classification. Persistent offenders, especially sex offenders, become the new lepers: diseased, incurable, unable to control outbreaks, themselves to blame for whatever privations society imposes upon them.

CHAPTER 3

Policy Issues

Introduction

This chapter considers policy issues that are raised by the preventive detention of sex offenders. Preventive detention regimes challenge human rights principles established in domestic and international law. We review the regimes in Queensland, Washington State and Scotland and consider to what extent they are compatible with these principles. This analysis commences in this chapter and concludes in Chapter 4, which focuses on the practical issues that have arisen from the implementation of the preventive detention regimes, particularly in Australia. Here, we examine some of the fundamental ideas that inform the different approaches that have been taken in the three jurisdictions.

At the outset, it is important to reinforce a number of fundamental points. First, no system of preventive detention, whether its dominant focus is community protection or psychological treatment (most systems involve both, and these objectives can overlap at any rate), will eliminate sexual offending. Second, it is impossible to contrive a perfect risk-free society through the law alone. Third, some people who have never offended may offend in the future, and preventive detention schemes cannot prevent these crimes. Fourth, some people who have previously offended may reoffend in the future contrary to predictions (as we observed in Chapter 2, risk prediction is an inexact science).

Preventive detention will never provide a perfect solution to the problem of sexual offending. Unless every sex offender is sent to prison for life regardless of the seriousness of the offence, governments will continue to be faced with the challenge of how to manage offenders when they are released from prison.

Should we lock all sex offenders up and throw away the key? This would protect the community from *convicted* sex offenders, but it would not stop sex offending. As set out in Chapter 2, most sex offences are committed by 'men connected to their victims as family or friends' (Gelb, 2007, p 10), and many sex offences are not reported or insufficient evidence is available to ensure criminal convictions. In Chapter 2, we also pointed out that the available research does not support the premise that sex offenders inevitably reoffend or that they are more likely to reoffend than other groups of offenders. To advocate that all convicted sex offenders should be imprisoned for life would ignore the range and level of seriousness of such offences. Should a flasher receive the same sentence as a violent rapist? Should a one-time offender be given the same sentence as a repeat offender? The resolution of the differences between the cases that are prosecuted involves questions of fact and degree and for the reasons that follow, require nuanced responses.

Traditionally, the differences between the seriousness of cases has been resolved by reference to the common law principle of proportionality: that the type and extent of punishment should be proportionate to the gravity of the harm and the degree of the offender's responsibility. The majority of the High Court of Australia in the case of *Veen v The Queen (No 2)* (1988) 164 CLR 465 at 472-475 confirmed that proportionality is the paramount principle in determining the length of criminal sentences. But the High Court also stated that the application of the principle of proportionality does not mean that public protection is irrelevant. The majority in *Veen (No 2)* drew a distinction between merely inflating a sentence for the purposes of preventive detention, which is not permissible, and exercising the sentencing discretion having regard to the protection of society among other factors, which is permissible. Robert Veen was an Aboriginal prostitute who suffered brain damage. In *Veen (No 2)* he was sentenced to life imprisonment for murder. Historically, a life term has been reserved for offenders for whom there are no prospects of rehabilitation. It is relatively rare to sentence a first-time murderer for life, but Veen had previously been sentenced to 12 years for manslaughter (*Veen v The Queen (No 1)* (1979) 143 CLR 458), and he had a long and violent criminal history. An order of life imprisonment, or an indefinite sentence, at the time of conviction may be justified on the basis that it is commensurate to the seriousness of the offence committed.

We explore the role of sentencing – particularly indefinite sentencing – in the management of high risk offenders in Chapter 5. Here it is sufficient to observe that the *post-sentence* preventive detention of high risk offenders sits uncomfortably with the principle that the punishment must be proportionate to the crime because imprisonment for what a person is likely to do is, by its very essence, predicated upon what may or may not occur in the future (McSherry, 2005, pp 94-98). Since the possibility exists that a predicted offence may never occur, which renders any consideration of the proportionality of the response meaningless, preventive detention is always an extraordinary step to take (Keyzer and Blay, 2006). Further, since the logic of preventive detention is that a detainee has the potential to offend if released, the concept permits indefinite detention as long as the detainer is able to 'prove' that the detainee has the *potential* to meet the detainer's predictions of what the detainee will do. But what constitutes acceptable, cogent evidence of 'dangerousness' (Campbell, 2003)? By its very nature, preventive detention allows for imprisonment of 'criminal types', rather than imprisonment for criminal conduct (McSherry, 2004).

Advocates of legal reform to ensure the continuing detention of serious sex offenders have expressed frustration at the inadequacy of the legal system in protecting the community. As one prominent Australian victim's rights advocate said, in response to the argument that Queensland's *Dangerous Prisoners (Sexual Offenders) Act 2003* (hence, the DPSOA) inflicts double punishment:

> What's happening here is we're just pussyfooting around. If what we're trying to do is to protect the community, protect innocent children, then let's do it. And if that means turning the law on its head, then let's do that too (Hetty Johnson, cited in Keyzer and Blay, 2006, p 410).

Where *should* the balance be struck between the right of the offender to liberty and the rights of society to be protected?

In a free society, the deprivation of liberty must always be justified (Magna Carta (1215), Articles 20 and 21). In *Chu Kheng Lim v Minister for Immigration* (1992) 176 CLR 1 at 27, Brennan, Deane and Dawson JJ, citing William Blackstone and AV Dicey, said:

> [T]he involuntary detention of a citizen in custody by the State is penal or punitive in character and, under our system of government, exists only as an incident of the exclusively judicial function of adjudging and punishing criminal guilt. Every citizen is 'ruled by the law, and by the law alone' and 'may with us be punished for a breach of law, but he can be punished for nothing else'.

Since the deprivation of liberty is always an extraordinary step to take, exceptions to this principle must be clearly justified. The effective rehabilitation of sex offenders provides a clear justification for continued detention. Acknowledging the many limitations of risk assessment outlined in Chapter 2, it would appear to us that the best system of preventive detention of high risk offenders would aim to eliminate reoffending with as minimal an impact on civil rights as possible.

In this chapter, we assess the policy settings in each of the three jurisdictions of Queensland, Washington State and Scotland with this balanced objective in mind. In making this assessment we need to be conscious of the differences in the architecture of rights in each of the three jurisdictions. This appears to have had a significant impact on regime design, particularly in Queensland.

Queensland

The Post-Sentence Detention and Supervision Model

In *Kable v Director of Public Prosecutions* (1995) 36 NSWLR 374 at 376, Justice Dennis Mahoney of the New South Wales Court of Appeal observed that preventive detention schemes 'may infringe - and certainly will create the danger of infringement of - the basic human rights which should underlie the laws of a modern democratic society'. The *Universal Declaration of Human Rights* recognises the 'inherent dignity and inalienable rights of all members of the human family' and sets out a series of rights as 'a common standard of achievement for all peoples and all nations'. The rights of prisoners and their entitlement to fairness in legal procedures are consolidated in a number of international instruments such as the United Nations *Standard Minimum Rules for the Treatment of Prisoners* and the United Nations *Convention Against Torture and Other Cruel, Inhuman or Degrading Treatment or Punishment*. The most relevant covenant to preventive detention schemes is the *International Covenant on Civil and Political Rights* (ICCPR) to which Australia is a signatory (signed 18 December 1972, ratified 13 August 1980). The relevant provisions in this covenant are discussed later in this chapter. The United Nations has also set out a number of rights for victims in its *Declaration of Basic Principles of Justice for Victims of Crime and Abuse of Power* (adopted by General Assembly resolution 40/34 of 29 November 1985).

An individual who has been a victim of a sexual offence suffers a terrible breach of his or her human rights. Victims of sexual offences can suffer serious and permanent psychological and emotional damage (see for example the comments of Justice Atkinson in *Pearce* [2005] QSC 314). The criminal justice system does little or nothing to remedy this breach, and serious questions can be raised about the adequacy of that system, or of criminal compensation laws, to do so.

However, in a study of the preventive detention of serious sex offenders, the focus shifts to the human rights of offenders, who, having served a criminal sentence, would otherwise be entitled to release and liberty unless they commit a new offence (see for example *Van Dessel* [2006] QSC 16 at [17]). Preventive detention, particularly where it takes place in a prison or in an institution with a punitive character, necessarily raises human rights issues.

Offenders do not forfeit their human rights when they commit a crime. In this respect, the DPSOA is unique because it demonstrates what is possible in a common law jurisdiction that is, to all extents and purposes, unencumbered by the requirement to protect human rights. Neither Queensland nor Australia has a constitutionally entrenched or statutory bill of rights. It is not accidental that none of the three Australian States that has opted for the preventive detention of sex offenders in prison (New South Wales, Queensland and Western Australia) has implemented statutory protection of human rights. Victoria and the Australian Capital Territory, on the other hand, which do have human rights protections through the Victorian *Charter of Human Rights and Responsibilities* and the *Human Rights Act 2004* (ACT) respectively, have not opted to reimprison serious sex offenders (although in Victoria, section 16(3A) of the *Serious Sex Offenders Monitoring Act 2005* (Vic) was introduced in 2006 to enable offenders under extended supervision orders to reside at premises 'within the perimeter of a prison').

The next sections deal with some of the important human rights principles that have been raised in relation to the Queensland preventive detention scheme.

Detention in Prison and Double Punishment

The DPSOA was subject to a constitutional challenge in *Fardon v Attorney-General (Qld)* (2004) 223 CLR 575. As set out in Chapter 1,

Robert John Fardon was the first person incarcerated under that Act. At the time the DPSOA was enacted, Fardon had three weeks left to serve in a 14-year sentence for rape. Fardon challenged the constitutional validity of the DPSOA on the ground that it authorised the Supreme Court to order the civil commitment of a person to prison without a fresh crime, or a trial or conviction for that crime, meaning that the law authorised double punishment. He argued that for these reasons, the law was inconsistent with the essential character of a court and, consequently, the separation of judicial power effected by the Australian Constitution (Keyzer, Pereira and Southwood, 2004).

The constitutional argument was based on the previous decision of the High Court of Australia in *Kable v Director of Public Prosecutions (NSW)* (1996) 189 CLR 51. In that case, a majority of the High Court struck down New South Wales legislation purporting to authorise the Supreme Court of New South Wales to order the preventive detention of Gregory Wayne Kable. Justice William Gummow, one of the members of the majority in that case, had observed (at 132):

> Whilst imprisonment pursuant to Supreme Court order is punitive in nature, it [was] not [made] consequent upon any adjudgment by the Court of criminal guilt. Plainly ... such an authority could not be conferred by a law of the Commonwealth upon this Court, any other federal court, or a State court exercising federal jurisdiction ... [N]ot only is such an authority non-judicial in nature, it is repugnant to the judicial process in a fundamental degree.

Justices John Toohey, Mary Gaudron and Michael McHugh (at 96-97, 106 and 120) also identified the imprisonment of a person not for what he or she had done but for what he or she might do as a factor leading to the conclusion that the legislation was unconstitutional (Keyzer, 2008, pp 104-105). The majority struck down the New South Wales law on the ground that it had imposed functions that were incompatible with the exercise of federal judicial power (Hanks, Keyzer and Clarke, 2004).

In *Fardon v Attorney-General (Qld)* (2004) 223 CLR 575 the High Court distinguished *Kable* on the basis that the legislation in that case was aimed at one person, Gregory Wayne Kable, who had been convicted of the manslaughter of his estranged wife, whereas the DPSOA refers to a class of prisoners, serious sex offenders. The double punishment argument was also rejected. A majority of the High Court of Australia held that detention in a prison is not correctly characterised as punishment if it is ordered for non-punitive reasons ((2004) 223 CLR 575 at 592, 597, 610, 647 and 654). Justices Ian Callinan and Dyson Heydon stated:

> [T]he [DPSOA], as the respondent submits, is intended to protect the community from predatory sexual offenders. It is a protective law authorising involuntary detention in the interests of public safety. Its proper characterisation is as a protective rather than a punitive enactment (at 654).

Justice Michael Kirby, who was the sole dissentient, said:

> Effectively, what is attempted involves the second court in reviewing, and increasing, the punishment previously imposed by the first court for precisely the same *past* conduct. Alternatively, it involves the second court in superimposing additional punishment on the basis that the original maximum punishment provided by law, as imposed, has later proved inadequate and that a new foundation for additional punishment, in effect retrospective, may be discovered in order to increase it (at 644).

The High Court's decision in *Fardon* opened the door to the other States to commence preventive detention in prison (McSherry, 2005), and New South Wales and Western Australia stepped through that door.

The High Court's decision in *Fardon* marked a radical shift in its approach to the character of imprisonment. Previously, in *Power v The Queen* (1974) 131 CLR 623 at 627, Chief Justice Garfield Barwick and Justices Douglas Menzies, Ninian Stephen and Anthony Mason stated:

> We cannot understand how ... imprisonment, either with or without hard labour, can, however enlightened the prison system is, be regarded as otherwise than a severe punishment.

In 1986, the Australian Human Rights Commission observed, perhaps optimistically, that 'until relatively recently it was generally accepted that one of the consequences of imprisonment was the extinction or suspension of basic civil rights' (Hawkins, 1986). 'Civil death' was seen as a necessary and indeed a desirable consequence of conviction: if an individual breaches fundamental criminal laws he or she is assumed to have rejected society, which must then reject that individual until he or she has been punished and rehabilitated. In 1969, Justice John Barry of the Supreme Court of Victoria observed (Barry, 1969):

> The public image of a prison as a place of degradation where it is right and proper that inmates should be repressed and debased is

> still strong. In the public mind … a prison is a place where people who have done wicked things are kept apart and held in subjection, so that they will not contaminate law-abiding citizens.

Despite the Australian Human Rights Commission's optimism, there is little evidence to indicate that the public has changed its opinions about the role and function of prison (Roberts and Indermaur, 2007; Jones, Weatherburn and Macfarlane, 2008). The overwhelming majority of Australians think that people who break the law should be given stiffer sentences (Roberts and Indermaur, 2007, and references there cited). The DPSOA has satisfied this popular demand for the retributive treatment of convicted sex offenders (Douglas, 2008).

An Australian who alleges that his or her human rights have been abused can petition the Human Rights Committee of the United Nations under the provisions of the *First Optional Protocol* to the *International Covenant on Civil and Political Rights*, which came into force in Australia on 25 December 1991. Robert Fardon has made such a petition to the Human Rights Committee (Keyzer and Blay 2006), and so has Kenneth Tillman, the first New South Wales resident (and first Aboriginal Australian) incarcerated under the *Crimes (Serious Sex Offenders) Act 2006* (NSW) (Keyzer, 2009a). While the opinions of the Human Rights Committee are not legally binding in Australia, they are taken seriously by many State parties, and have been implemented by the Australian government in a number of instances.

The *Fardon* and *Tillman* communications have raised arguments under Articles 9(1) and 14(7) of the ICCPR. Article 9(1) provides:

> Everyone has the right to liberty and security of the person. No one shall be subjected to arbitrary arrest or detention. No one shall be deprived of his [or her] liberty except on such grounds and in accordance with such procedure as are established by law.

The meaning of the term 'arbitrary' in this passage is open to debate. On a narrow view, the article could mean that arbitrary detention denotes not according to legislative procedure (Blay and Piotrowicz, 2001). However, Claire Macken (2005) has argued that arbitrary detention means more than 'unlawful' detention. It imposes an additional higher requirement above unlawfulness. That is, 'arbitrary' could be taken to mean unreasonable or unjust. Exploring the background travaux préparatoires of the ICCPR, Parvez Hassan (1973) reveals that the drafters gave a distinct meaning to the word. He points out (p 179) that in the Report of the Third Committee, the majority stated that an arbitrary act was one that violated justice, reason *or* legislation.

While Kenneth Tillman's reimprisonment was 'on such grounds and in accordance with such procedure as are established by law', the lawfulness of his detention within Australia is not determinative of whether or not the detention was arbitrary and a breach of Article 9. The jurisprudence of the Human Rights Committee provides that to avoid being characterised as arbitrary, detention must be (a) 'reasonable', (b) 'necessary in all the circumstances of the case' and (c) 'proportionate to achieving the legitimate ends of the State party' (Keyzer, 2009a). In addition, if a State is able to achieve its legitimate ends by a means less invasive than detention, detention will be considered to be arbitrary (Keyzer, 2009a).

The legislative objectives of the *Crimes (Serious Sex Offenders) Act 2006* (NSW) as set out in section 3 – '(a) to ensure the safety and protection of the community, and (b) to facilitate the rehabilitation of serious sex offenders' – are legitimate ones. Kenneth Tillman explicitly accepted this in his communication to the United Nations Human Rights Committee. However, Robert Fardon and Kenneth Tillman have disputed the legitimacy of using reimprisonment to achieve those objectives (Keyzer, 2009a). Fardon and Tillman have argued that imprisonment is a disproportionate response to the legitimate end of rehabilitating sex offenders; that a purpose-designed facility focusing on treatment and/or supervision in the community with treatment supports would have satisfied the requirements of Article 9.

The second human rights argument raised in the *Fardon* and *Tillman* communications is based on Article 14(7) of the *International Covenant on Civil and Political Rights*, which provides:

> No one shall be liable to be tried or punished again for an offence for which he has already been finally convicted or acquitted in accordance with the law and penal procedure of each country.

There are no decisions of the United Nations Human Rights Committee that have considered the use of prison for preventive detention after a sentence has been served; the *Fardon* and *Tillman* communications are the first. However, there was some discussion of the principle of double punishment in the minority opinion in *Rameka v New Zealand* (No 1090/2002, 15 December 2003). In that communication, the applicants, three repeat sex offenders, challenged New Zealand's statutory provisions authorising a court to order indefinite sentences for their most recent offences. The provisions allowed the court to take into account materials predicting whether the men would be a danger to society if released. The offenders complained to the United Nations Human Rights Committee that:

> [I]t was arbitrary to impose a discretionary sentence on the basis of evidence of future dangerousness, as such a conclusion cannot satisfy the statutory tests of 'substantial risk of re-offending' or 'expedient for the protection of the public' in the individual case. ... [O]n the facts none of them fit the statutory tests of being a 'substantial risk', [nor was] preventive detention ... 'expedient for protection of the public' (*Rameka* at [3.2]).

The focus of the majority decision was on the opportunity for periodic review of preventive detention. The majority opinion stated:

> The Committee considers that the ... authors' detention for preventive purposes, that is, protection of the public, once a punitive term of imprisonment has been served, must be justified by compelling reasons, reviewable by a judicial authority, that are and remain applicable as long as detention for these purposes continues (*Rameka* at [7.3]).

The Committee concluded it had not been demonstrated that the future operation of the sentences the complainants had begun to serve would amount to arbitrary detention, contrary to Article 9, once the preventive aspect of their sentences commenced (*Rameka* at [7.3]). Since preventive detention had been imposed by the courts *at the time of conviction* in each of the three cases before the courts, the issues of double punishment and the consistency of preventive detention with Article 14(7) understandably did not arise (Keyzer and Blay, 2006).

This presents a fundamental difference that strengthens *Fardon* and *Tillman's* communications. The very essence of these communications is that, unlike the cases in New Zealand, the preventive detention was not imposed as part of, or in the context of, the same criminal trial process that imposed the initial finite sentence. Fardon's reimprisonment took place outside and independent of the initial criminal trial and after the completion of the finite sentence, without a finding of any new grounds of guilt. On this basis, it can be argued that this constitutes double punishment for the initial offence. As Justice Kirby noted in *Fardon*, the DPSOA 'involves a later judge being required, in effect, to impose new punishment beyond that fixed by an earlier judge, without any intervening offence, trial or conviction' (*Fardon v Attorney-General (Qld)* (2004) 223 CLR 575 at 643-644 [182]).

The minority of judges in *Rameka v New Zealand* acknowledged the danger of such an approach. Although double jeopardy was not raised by the New Zealand communication, the minority did address the issue:

> [I]t is the very principle of detention based solely on potential dangerousness that [we] challenge, especially as detention of this kind often carries on from, and becomes a mere and, it would not be going too far to say, an 'easy' extension of a penalty of imprisonment ... While often presented as precautionary, measures of the kind in question are in reality penalties, and this change of their original nature constitutes a means of circumventing the provisions of articles 14 and 15 of the [ICCPR] (Individual Opinion of Mr Prafullachandra Natwarlal Bhagwati, Ms Christine Chanet, Mr Glèlè Ahanhanzo and Mr Hipólito Solari Yrigoye, dissenting in part).

The minority observations represent the only Committee statement on double punishment to date. At the time of writing, final submissions had been filed by the parties and a decision of the UNHRC was still pending. Christopher Slobogin (2006, p 112) has written:

> Criminal punishment is based solely on a conviction for an offense [sic] and can occur only if there is such a conviction. Preventive detention is based solely on a prediction concerning future offenses [sic] and can occur only if there is such a prediction. Therefore, preventive detention is not punishment.

That observation must, however, be qualified because it emerges from the United States context. In the United States of America, civil commitment is intended to take place in purpose-designed facilities that are not *supposed to be* prisons. However, as explored in Chapter 4, many observers would argue that the United States civil commitment regime merely authorises imprisonment under a different guise. In *Kansas v Hendricks* 521 US 346 (1997), the leading United States authority confirming the constitutionality of civil commitment regimes, Justice Clarence Thomas, writing for the majority (of five), characterised the Kansas sexually violent predator law by reference to the motives of the legislature, expressed to be to commit sex offenders for (only) non-punitive reasons.

The real question that underlies the principle of double punishment is whether or not the preventive detention ordered *and experienced* amounts to punishment. Justice Stephen Breyer, for the minority (of four) in *Kansas v Hendricks*, said that it is the actual operation of the law that counts and, if it is punitive, then it should be declared unconstitutional (Carlsmith, Monahan and Evans, 2007). The United States Supreme Court had previously emphasised this requirement in *Allen v Illinois* 478 US 364 (1986). Acknowledging that the laws in New South Wales, Queensland and Western Australia return offenders to *prison*, it is difficult to accept that post-sentence reimprisonment does not constitute double punishment, even if it is ordered for other non-punitive purposes. While preventive detention schemes may omit any mention of punishment, if imprisonment is punishment, the effect of an order merely labelled 'detention' is precisely that (Keyzer, 2008).

Proportionality and Finality of Sentence

The resolution of the question whether reimprisonment under the DPSOA constitutes double punishment has a bearing on the resolution of a number of other policy issues relating to the DPSOA (and similar legislation in New South Wales and Western Australia). Post-sentence preventive detention, whether it takes place in a prison or in a special commitment centre, is based on what the offender might do in the future and is in that sense disconnected from the offence committed, which led to the period of imprisonment. It might therefore be argued that post-sentence preventive detention offends against the principle of proportionality in sentencing (Keyzer, Pereira and Southwood, 2004). On the other hand, because preventive detention regimes are based on what offenders might do, it could be argued that the principle of proportionality is simply irrelevant, at least where an offender has not been returned to a punitive environment. Preventive detention is the *only* certain way to ensure that an offender will not pose any risk to the community. Questions of proportionality therefore only arise if the detention is punitive in character.

Post-sentence preventive detention legislation that authorises imprisonment may be seen as contrary to the principle of finality of sentence (Warner 2003, p 338; Keyzer, Pereira and Southwood, 2004; McSherry, 2005). If an order for indefinite detention or lifelong restriction is made at the time of the sentence (as in *Rameka v New Zealand* or in the Scottish regime we discuss below), then the offender at least knows that there is a nominal term and a system for periodic review. By contrast, post-sentence preventive detention schemes operate at the end of the offender's sentence, leading to uncertainty as to how long the offender must remain in prison after the sentence expires. This uncertainty may be exacerbated by the irregular timing of periodic reviews (Keyzer and O'Toole, 2006), some of which may only take place years after the offender has been reimprisoned (Keyzer and Coyle, 2009). Again, the principle of finality in sentencing may be considered irrelevant if it is accepted that post-sentence preventive detention is not punitive.

Retrospective Operation

There is a possibility, noted by Justice Michael Kirby in *Fardon v Attorney-General (Qld)* (2004) 223 CLR 575, that the DPSOA is a criminal law that operates retrospectively because it inflicts further punishment without a criminal trial. There is a general legal principle that legislation which criminalises certain conduct or sets up sentencing regimes should not apply retrospectively. Article 15(1) of the *International Covenant on Civil and Political Rights* states: 'No one shall be held guilty of any criminal offence on account of any act or omission which did not constitute a criminal offence, under national or international law, at the time when it was committed'. Justice John Toohey explained the rationale for this principle in *Polyukhovich v Commonwealth* (1991) 172 CLR 501 at 688-689:

> Protection against retroactive laws protects a particular accused against potentially capricious state action. But the principle also represents a protection of a public interest. This is so, first, in the sense that every individual is, by the principle, assured that no future retribution by society can occur except by reference to rules presently known; and secondly, it serves to promote a just society by encouraging a climate of security and humanity.

While the United States Constitution prohibits retrospective criminal laws (called *ex post facto* (from the Latin for 'after the fact') legislation in that jurisdiction), the majority in *Polyukhovich* confirmed there are no similar constitutional limits in Australia. Again, the validity of this argument depends on the conclusion that imprisonment is punishment. It could be argued that preventive detention schemes do not set up new criminal offences and therefore do not impose additional punishment where the purpose of such schemes is community protection. On this view, the principle of retrospectivity does not apply.

The Queensland Court of Appeal has countenanced circumstances in which a person's detention, though initially ordered for preventive reasons, could be truly punitive in operation. This might justify a judicial conclusion that the executive government had repudiated its preventive objectives and lead to a refusal to make an order detaining a person again. In *Attorney-General (Qld) v Francis* [2006] QCA 324, Justices Patrick Keane, Catherine Holmes and Peter Dutney stated at [31]:

> It is possible ... that executive government repudiation of the preventive objects of the Act in a particular case (as, for example, by the refusal of treatment to a prisoner clearly capable of, and amenable to, rehabilitation) could lead the court to refuse to make any order at all. If it were to appear to the court that any further detention would be truly punitive in character and, thus, contrary to the intention of the legislation, there would be no basis for the court to make an order of any kind under the Act. The conditions of further restraint upon the detainee's liberty would be out of character with the intention of the legislature: that such restraint is preventive.

On this view, the punitive character of the DPSOA does not arise from the fact that the detention takes place in a prison, but because the government might fail to provide treatment to a person who wants it. But it is difficult to see how such an argument can be advanced when the DPSOA authorises the Supreme Court of Queensland to make orders for the care *or* the treatment *or* the control of offenders. We explore the implications of this statement further when we examine the practical operation of the DPSOA in Chapter 4.

The Liberty Principle

Assuming that the DPSOA is compatible with the *International Covenant on Civil and Political Rights*, the rights of the offender can only be protected by statutory or common law principles. Two fundamental common law principles have been invoked in the DPSOA cases to aid in its construction. The first principle is that the right to personal liberty is the most elementary and important of all common law rights – it cannot be impaired or taken away without lawful authority and then only to the extent and for the time prescribed by law (*Williams v The Queen* (1986) 161 CLR 278 at 292, cited by Justice Roslyn Atkinson in *Fardon* [2003] QSC 331 at [19]). As Justice Margaret White observed in *Van Dessel* [2006] QSC 16 at [17], what is at stake is a person's fundamental legal right to unfettered personal liberty on the expiration of his term of imprisonment (see also *Downs* [2008] QSC 87 at [28], *Taylor* [2008] QSC 183 at [29] and *Carpenter* [2008] QSC 225 at [7]). Accordingly, legislation that has the effect of derogating from the right of an individual to enjoy liberty is, in the case of ambiguity, accorded a strict construction (*Coco v The Queen* (1994) 179 CLR 427 at 437). On this basis the Queensland Court of Appeal held in *Francis* [2006] QCA 324 at [39]:

> The [DPSOA] does not contemplate that arrangements to prevent such a risk must be 'watertight'; otherwise [supervision] orders ... would never be made. The question is whether the protection of the community is adequately ensured. If supervision of the prisoner is apt to ensure adequate protection, having regard to the risk to the community posed by the prisoner, then an order for supervised release should, in principle, be preferred to a continuing detention order on the basis that the intrusions of the [DPSOA] upon the liberty of the subject are exceptional, and the liberty of the subject should be constrained to no greater extent than is warranted by the statute which authorised such constraint.

The common law principle favouring liberty does not override the court's paramount concern for the protection of the community (*Waghorn* [2006] QSC 171 at [24]). But the liberty principle, applied by the Court of Appeal in *Francis*, has led the Supreme Court to prefer supervision orders to continuing detention orders in a majority of the cases that have been decided under the DPSOA.

Procedural Fairness

The second principle invoked in the DPSOA cases to condition the interpretation of the Act is the principle of procedural fairness. It provides legitimacy to the criminal justice process by maintaining a balance between the coercive powers of the State and the human rights of citizens of the State (Bronitt and McSherry, 2005, p 94). The principle of procedural fairness is relevant to any scheme that seeks to supervise or preventively detain high risk offenders because it requires safeguards to ensure that hearings carried out under the scheme operate in a way that is fair to the person being detained or supervised. Such safeguards could include periodic reviews, rights of appeal and access to an independent tribunal. Given that imprisonment is the most serious consequence of a judicial decision, procedural fairness requirements must be taken into account in the post-sentence preventive detention context (*Watego* (2003) 142 A Crim R 537).

Two cases have considered the requirements of procedural fairness in relation to the Queensland scheme of preventive detention (*Watego* (2003) 142 A Crim R 537; *Nash* (2003) 143 A Crim R 312). Both cases have held that procedural fairness requires that prisoners have adequate time to prepare for their hearings, to instruct counsel, to analyse quantities of evidentiary material and to make arrangements for witnesses to give evidence (Keyzer and O'Toole, 2006). In *Watego* (2003) 142 A Crim R 537, the Queensland Court of Appeal dismissed an appeal against a decision to dismiss an application for preventive detention. The application had been brought against the prisoner within a very short period of time before his release. Because of the prisoner's detention and the problems he faced in securing legal representation, the court dismissed the application on the basis that the prisoner was denied procedural fairness as he did not have appropriate time to prepare a sufficient defence. In *Nash* (2003) 143 A Crim R 312, an application for preventive detention was also brought only days before the release date of the prisoner. As in *Watego's* case, the court dismissed the application on the basis that the prisoner was denied procedural fairness.

One uncertainty that operates in this area relates to the status of the principles of procedural fairness or due process principles generally as a source of restriction on legislative power (as distinct from executive power). The doctrine of procedural fairness is derived from the common law and, in Australia, principles of procedural fairness have been applied by the High Court within the framework of its jurisdiction to issue 'constitutional writs'.

In *Fardon's* case a number of the majority judges analysed the Queensland law in terms of its consistency with 'judicial process', inferring that 'judicial process' may provide a yardstick against which the DPSOA and similar legislation can be tested. The contours of 'judicial process' are as yet indistinct, but it may be observed that a majority of the High Court in *Fardon's* case emphasised that the retention and application of rules of evidence under the DPSOA was of some significance to a conclusion that the 'process' authorised by the DPSOA was appropriately 'judicial'. It is conceivable that inappropriate variations to the rules of evidence, which adversely affect procedural fairness under such regimes, might warrant judicial reconsideration of the constitutional validity of post-sentence preventive detention regimes. However, it should also be noted that the High Court has previously accepted that legislatures have wide power to vary the rules of evidence in criminal cases (Keyzer, 2005, p 273).

In the absence of a decision in the *Fardon* and *Tillman* communications, the normative boundaries of preventive detention regimes in Australia presently depend on the imagination of State Attorneys-General and their legal advisers.

Washington State

The Inpatient (But Rarely Outpatient) Model

As we observed in Chapter 2, many of the States of the United States of America (Texas is one exception) have adopted 'inpatient' civil commitment regimes that involve post-sentence confinement of 'sexually violent predators' in a detention centre staffed by mental health professionals and security staff. These commitment regimes are expressed to be for the rehabilitation of offenders, who can petition the State at any time for re-entry into society. Re-entry to the community, when it takes place, is often accompanied by restrictions on freedom of movement and monitoring in the community. Washington State's Sexually Violent Predator Law was the first of its kind in the United States and it has served as a model for most other United States sexually violent predator legislation. It provides a convenient model for comparative study because it is 'the only program in the [United States] in which the constitutional parameters of the treatment program have been fully litigated' (Smith, 2008).

Like Queensland's DPSOA, the Washington State law authorises post-sentence detention by way of civil commitment, and therefore without a number of the protections available in the criminal justice system. Like the DPSOA, the United States inpatient systems have been criticised for authorising double punishment and for extending prison terms indefinitely, thereby distorting the principle of proportionality that should be applied in sentencing. As the United States has a constitutionally entrenched Bill of Rights, the resolution of many of the significant challenges that post-sentence preventive detention pose to civil rights have been considered by the United States Supreme Court (Janus, 2000; La Fond, 2000). The constitutional parameters have largely been worked out in three cases (*Allen v Illinois* 478 US 364 (1986); *Kansas v Hendricks* 521 US 346 (1997) and *Seling v Young* 531 US 250 (2001)).

In *Allen v Illinois* 478 US 364 (1986), the United States Supreme Court upheld Illinois legislation that authorised the civil commitment of 'sexually dangerous persons' to a psychiatric institution for care and treatment. In the course of the proceedings, the State of Illinois presented the evidence of two examining psychiatrists, who testified that Terry Allen had a mental disorder and a propensity to commit sexual assaults. Allen objected on the ground that his Fifth Amendment privilege against self-incrimination had been violated. The Appellate Court of Illinois for the Third District reversed the trial court's finding that Allen was a sexually dangerous person. The Supreme Court of Illinois then unanimously reversed the Appellate Court finding and reinstated the trial court's finding (481 NE 2d 690 (1985)). It held that the privilege against self-incrimination was not available in sexually dangerous person proceedings, because such proceedings were 'essentially civil in nature'. The aim of the Illinois law was to provide treatment, not inflict punishment (at 694-695). The Supreme Court granted certiorari, and affirmed the judgment of the Supreme Court of Illinois.

The Fifth Amendment provides that no person 'shall be compelled in any criminal case to be a witness against himself'. The Fourteenth Amendment of the United States Constitution (also called the 'due process clause') states in part:

> No State shall make or enforce any law which shall abridge the privileges or immunities of citizens of the United States; nor shall any State deprive any person of life, liberty, or property, without due process of law; nor deny to any person within its jurisdiction the equal protection of the laws.

The due process clause has been interpreted as applying the Fifth Amendment to the States (*Malloy v Hogan* 378 US 1 (1964)). In *Malloy* the Supreme Court had held that the Fifth Amendment 'not only permits a person to refuse to testify against himself at a criminal trial in which he is a defendant', but also 'privileges him not to answer official questions put to him in any other proceeding, civil or criminal, formal or informal, where the answers might incriminate him in future criminal proceedings'.

The majority of the Supreme Court in *Allen v Illinois* (Rehnquist J, writing for Burger CJ, White, Powell and O'Connor JJ) distinguished *Malloy* on the basis that the proceedings under the Illinois law were not criminal in nature nor in their effect. The Supreme Court accepted Illinois' submissions that the legislation was passed for non-punitive (preventive) reasons. The Supreme Court accepted that the text of the challenged statute would not be 'dispositive' of the question whether the law was punitive or not, and that the court could have regard to the actual effect of the law in making its judgment whether or not the law was criminal in nature. On this score, the majority held that Allen had failed to prove that commitment to a purpose-designed psychiatric institution for care and treatment was punitive. Allen argued that his civil commitment was punitive because the psychiatric institution in question would house people who had been subject to civil commitment orders along with criminals who had psychiatric problems. Justice William Rehnquist, for the majority, said that Allen had

> not demonstrated, and the record does not suggest, that 'sexually dangerous persons' in Illinois are confined under conditions incompatible with the State's asserted interest in treatment. Had petitioner shown, for example, that the confinement of such persons imposes on them a regimen which is essentially identical to that imposed upon felons with no need for psychiatric care, this might well be a different case. But the record here tells us little or nothing about the regimen at the psychiatric center, and it certainly does not show that there are no relevant differences between confinement there and confinement in the other parts of the maximum security prison complex. Indeed, counsel for the State assures us that, under Illinois law, sexually dangerous persons must not be treated like ordinary prisoners. Tr of Oral Arg 32-33. We therefore cannot say that the conditions of petitioner's confinement themselves amount to 'punishment,' and thus render 'criminal' the proceedings which led to confinement.

Justice John Stevens, for the minority (also comprising Brennan, Marshall and Blackmun JJ), held that the law was unconstitutional because the proceedings could not take place without the anterior commission of a sexual offence for which the person had already been punished. This was explained on the grounds that indefinite detention in a psychiatric institution was a very significant deprivation of liberty and because a finding that a person was a sexually dangerous person was as stigmatising as concluding that he or she was a criminal. Justice Stevens concluded with a criticism of the majority judgment in the following terms (at 383):

> For the Court, these concerns are not implicated today because the prosecution-initiated and prison-destined, sexually dangerous person proceeding is not 'criminal' in nature. In my opinion, permitting a State to create a shadow criminal law without the fundamental protection of the Fifth Amendment conflicts with the respect for liberty and individual dignity that has long characterized, and that continues to characterize, our free society.

In *Kansas v Hendricks* 521 US 346 (1997), the Kansas legislation that was similar to Washington's sexually violent predator law was found to be constitutional. The case concerned the Kansas *Sexually Violent Predator Act*, which provided for the civil commitment of sex offenders who had a 'mental abnormality or personality disorder' that caused them to commit 'predatory acts of sexual violence'. Leroy Hendricks had an extensive criminal history of sexual offending against girls and boys including strangers and family members. Hendricks challenged the constitutional validity of the Kansas statute under the due process clause on the ground that it failed to require a finding of mental illness that might justify commitment; the statute instead required a (mere) finding of 'mental abnormality' or 'personality disorder'.

The Supreme Court upheld the statute by a majority of five justices to four. They noted that Hendricks had been diagnosed as a paedophile, and that this could credibly be described as a mental abnormality. The majority did not find that 'due process' required a finding of mental *illness* per se, rather that civil confinement must be preceded by an adjudication that proved the person in question was dangerous and that he or she suffered from a volitional impairment rendering him or her dangerous. The majority held that the law was not punitive in intent or effect, and, further, that incapacitation could, in and of itself, be a legitimate end (at 365-368). Treatment need only be provided where a condition was treatable (at 366). Justice Stephen Breyer, with whom Justices John Stevens and David Souter joined (Justice Ruth Bader Ginsburg joining in part), noted that Kansas had failed to provide for less restrictive alternatives, such as post-release supervision or placement in a residential facility with therapeutic supports.

In 2002, the Supreme Court of the United States subsequently limited the application of the Kansas law to those having 'serious difficulty in controlling behaviour' (*Kansas v Crane* 534 US 407 (2002)). The Supreme Court of the United States has also found the Washington scheme to be civil in nature (*Seling v Young* 531 US 250 (2001)). This case concerned Andre Brigham Young, who had been detained under the Washington law after the conclusion of his sentence for six rapes. Young argued that while the law might be valid on its face, it was punitive in its effect. He urged the Court to apply the approach to the characterisation of the law that was endorsed by the majority of the Court in *Allen v Illinois* – that it was necessary for the Court to recognise the practical effect of the legislation, which was to detain people indefinitely in prison-style conditions. The majority held that the clearest proof of punitive conditions would be required to disprove the legislature's stated intention, and that Allen had not satisfied that burden. The majority accepted the stated objectives of Washington's law as preventive and rehabilitative (Thampy, 2004) and found that the civil commitment regime did not offend the constitutional guarantees against *ex post facto* legislation and double jeopardy (Presley, 1999).

Following the cases of *Hendricks* and *Seling*, State legislatures have been careful not to draft legislation that appears to be punitive. Instead, the laws are expressed to be preventive measures to reduce the risk posed by dangerous offenders rather than to serve as punishment for specific crimes. The majority in *Seling* noted that the Washington State law required adequate care and individualised treatment, and that detainees were at liberty to bring civil suits to enforce Washington State's statutory obligations to provide this care and treatment. The Court specifically noted that Washington State's special commitment centre for sex offenders was operating subject to an injunction issued by the Federal District Court in Washington State that required it to provide such care and treatment.

In the next chapter, we explore the impact of this injunction on the operation of the Washington State regime. It will be argued that it has had a negligible impact. Lawyers representing detainees under the Washington State system have argued persuasively that without adequate treatment providing a path to an individual's potential release, civil commitment becomes state-imposed criminal punishment, yet a civilly committed individual lacks the procedural protections typically afforded a criminal defendant (Smith, 2008). It is difficult to avoid the conclusion that the United States' sexually violent predator laws have had a punitive effect (Willis, 2008). Few sex offenders detained under these laws have been released (La Fond, 2005). The constitutional requirement that civil commitment be authorised for treatment has often not been fulfilled. The general recalcitrance of government officials to provide constitutionally adequate treatment suggests that civil commitment was never intended to rehabilitate offenders, but to warehouse potentially dangerous offenders after their sentences have ended (Smith, 2008).

There have been many extra-constitutional objections to the United States inpatient regimes. First, some sex offenders are not, by psychiatric standards, mentally ill (Willis, 2008) and the belief that the majority of sex offenders are mentally ill is not supported by research (Lievore, 2005). The term 'paedophile' has been conflated to mean 'sex offender' in general parlance, whereas 'paedophile' is used much more narrowly in the American Psychiatric Association's Fourth Diagnostic and Statistical Manual of Mental Disorders (DSM-IV-TR, 2000) to refer to the 'paraphilia' (a sexual deviation) of being sexually attracted primarily or exclusively to children. Only a small subset of sex offenders is diagnosed with this form of sexual deviation.

If there is no mental health rationale for further detention after the conclusion of a criminal sentence, this reinforces the civil libertarian argument that preventive detention has been ordered purely for the purpose of social control (Janus, 2004; Hayes, 2009). Mental health professionals in the United States have pointed to and criticised the use of the term 'mental abnormality' – a broader category than 'mental illness' – in civil commitment legislation. They argue that the term 'mental abnormality' contemplates further detention without a diagnosis of psychiatric illness that historically provided the justification for commitment to a mental health facility (Winick and La Fond, 2003; Keyzer, Pereira and Southwood, 2004). Once the criteria for preventive detention have expanded beyond matters capable of psychiatric assessment, the spectre of value judgments by reference to vague ideas emerges. As Paul Appelbaum (1997b, p 1265) has observed in relation to the criteria in the Kansas statute (which copied the Washington statute), this 'makes it likely that those offenders committed under this statute will be a heterogeneous group diagnostically similar only in the fears they arouse among authorities as their release approaches'.

For these reasons, the use of civil commitment to detain sex offenders has been criticised as representing nothing more than the transferral of preventive detention from the criminal to the civil system (Schneider, 1995). It raises the spectre of the abuse of the mental health care system to warehouse those with a 'mental abnormality' rather than a properly diagnosable and treatable mental illness.

Bruce Winick (2003) has also pointed to the phenomenon that the 'inpatient' medical model may ironically undermine treatment efforts for sex offenders who do not have a diagnosed mental illness. For example, he states that labelling individuals as violent sexual predators communicates to them that they are mentally abnormal in ways that prevent them from controlling their behaviour and may undermine the potential of any treatment offered (2003, p 321).

The same criticism can be levelled at community notification laws. By concentrating treatment endeavours for mental abnormality after imprisonment, there are disincentives for sex offenders to take advantage of prison treatment programs. A system whereby sex offenders are forced to undergo mandatory treatment in mental health institutions after their sentence may also have a negative impact on mental health professionals. Coercive treatment programs raise ethical problems and may be more concerned with social control than working in the best interests of the individual concerned. A system that threatens further detention to secure compliance with state mandated treatment objectives would appear to be susceptible to this criticism.

The treatment of confined individuals is of utmost importance in ensuring that sexual predator commitment programs are not abused as a mere device for incapacitating offenders (Ra, 2007). A 1999 review of six sexually violent predator programs in different States suggested than an average of 44 per cent of detainees refused treatment participation; at Atascadero, in California, the rate of treatment refusal was much higher (Hennessey, 1999). This raises questions regarding the management of treatment obligations and calls into question the use of significant resources to fund clinical programs in which prisoners decline to participate (Vess, 2005). The use of the mental health system to detain sex offenders may limit the availability of resources for the treatment of individuals with mental illnesses who have not offended (Smith, 2008). Targeting all sex offenders, most of whom are not dangerous, diverts limited resources away from the treatment of serious sex offenders (La Fond, 2005, p 57). It also fuels public hysteria that is unnecessary and counterproductive (La Fond, 2005, p 57).

While Washington State's civil commitment regime can be questioned for many reasons, it should not be isolated from its context. In 1984 Washington State enacted the Special Sex Offender Sentencing Alternative (SSOSA) Law. This allows first-time sex offenders to seek community treatment instead of incarceration. It has been argued that this sentencing alternative is essential to encourage offenders to report their crimes and access treatment (Berliner et al, 1991).

The United States inpatient regimes have been justified on the basis that: they enable the confinement of people who are sick and dangerous; they provide a venue for the exploitation of developing expertise in the treatment of sex offenders; they increase public safety, provide due process and protect future victims (La Fond, 2005, p 137). However, the unwillingness of the United States Supreme Court to provide effective constitutional protection of due process in this context has neutralised the capacity of inferior courts to compel the States to provide treatment and expend energy and resources on the effective rehabilitation of sex offenders.

Scotland

The Sentence of Lifelong Restriction Model

Scotland has adopted a hybrid, rather than a purely medical or criminal justice, model for the management of high risk offenders. The scheme recommended by the MacLean Committee (2000) and supported by the Scottish Executive (2001) allows for an order for lifelong restriction (OLR) to be placed on those who pose a continuing risk to the public. As outlined in Chapter 1, an OLR can only be made by the High Court and as part of a sentence. The sentence can apply for conviction for a single offence, but only if the offence is of a serious, violent or life endangering nature and the court is satisfied that the offender meets the statutory risk criteria. Under section 210E of the *Criminal Procedure (Scotland) Act 1995*, the risk criteria justifying the making of an OLR are as follows:

> that the nature of, or the circumstances of the commission of, the offence of which the convicted person has been found guilty either in themselves or as part of a pattern of behaviour are such as to

> demonstrate that there is a likelihood that he [or she], if at liberty, will seriously endanger the lives, or physical or psychological well-being, of members of the public at large.

The OLR commences in a custodial setting. The offenders are then released under supervision, subject to monitoring and restriction within the community. The Scottish regime has a focus on treatment, and contemplates staged release into the community following a structured and carefully administered risk assessment process.

The Risk Management Authority (RMA) has a key role in the OLR process. An executive non-departmental public body set up by section 3 of the *Criminal Justice (Scotland) Act 2003*, its role is to help protect the public by promoting and supporting high quality professional practice in managing the risk of serious harm presented by violent and sexual offenders. The Scottish Executive (2001, p 8) clarified that while the Authority would be funded by the government, it would be 'operationally independent'.

The Risk Management Authority: disseminates information regarding risk assessment and management; commissions research; accredits task centres for formal assessments; sets training standards for assessment; formulates risk management plans and commissions appropriate risk management services (Risk Management Authority, 2009a). The Risk Management Authority has set up specialist services for high risk offenders and intensive supervision and surveillance (Darjee and Crichton, 2002).

The Risk Management Authority's Standards and Guidelines (2007) are extraordinarily comprehensive and its *Risk Assessment Tools Evaluation Directory* (2007), which is referred to as 'RATED', not only provides an overview of risk assessment inventories, but points out the advantages and disadvantages of each. This directory emphasises (p 1) that risk assessment 'as an exercise is more than the application of risk assessment tools'.

The Scottish Executive (2001) envisaged that the Risk Management Authority would go beyond providing training and standards for risk assessment in relation to those on orders for lifelong restriction. It stated (p 12) that the Risk Management Authority would 'be able to co-ordinate a common approach to developing techniques and principles which will be incorporated within a common standards framework and used by all the agencies operating in this area of the criminal justice system'. This certainly seems to be occurring as its

Standard and Guidelines (2007) are now being used widely within the Scottish Prison Service.

A risk management plan is a personal plan for every offender who is sentenced to an OLR. It is modified and adapted to reflect the offender's risk and needs throughout his or her lifetime, whether in custody or in the community. The risk management plan is drawn up by the Scottish Prison Service and reviewed and changed as required during custody. If the offender is released into the community under supervision, responsibility for the plan will transfer to the local authority who will be responsible for supervising the offender in the community. The Risk Management Authority currently approves each plan and/or variations (Scottish Government News, 2006), but this may be delegated if the number of offenders subject to OLRs continues to rise.

Risk assessment reports, which need to be compiled according to the rigorous standards of the Risk Management Authority using structured professional (or clinical) judgment, raise the possibility that mental health professionals will err on the side of caution in terms of assessing the level of risk. Some mental health professionals might construe the option of an OLR as being indirectly beneficial to an offender in that he or she will have an individually tailored risk management plan aimed at minimising the risks of reoffending (assuming the offender is released from custody). If the offender does not reoffend then there will be no risk of further punishment by the criminal justice system, which is to the offender's and society's benefit (Tuddenham and Baird, 2007).

The role of risk assessor is a step further on from the traditional role of the forensic mental health professional who provides a medical report to the court. The risk assessment report on an offender is requested solely for judicial purposes, to determine what risk the offender's being 'at liberty presents to the safety of the public at large' (section 210B(3)). Unlike the Washington scheme, there is no requirement that any risk be linked to a mental disorder for the court to make an OLR. It is a sentencing option, but one that recognises that offenders may need treatment and supervision for life.

The Scottish approach was discussed at length by the MacLean Committee, which recommended the establishment of the Risk Management Authority. There has been no adverse comment in the mental health journals to date, which contrasts sharply with widespread criticism of the English and Welsh proposals for the detention of 'dangerous people with severe personality disorders' as mentioned in Chapter 2 (Mullen, 1999; Buchanan and Leese, 2001; Cordess, 2002; Moran, 2002; White, 2002; Tuddenham and Baird, 2007).

Scotland, being part of the United Kingdom, is subject to the human rights principles enunciated in the *European Convention on Human Rights* (ECHR). The Convention was opened to European nations for signature on 4 November 1950 in Rome, and it entered into force on 3 September 1953. The United Kingdom was one of the first signatories in 1951. However, it was not until 1998 that the United Kingdom ratified the articles of this convention into domestic law (EDA Secretariat, 2009). This was done via the *Human Rights Act 1998*, an Act which, as published upon receipt of Royal Assent on 9 November 1998, stated its purpose was to 'give further effect to rights and freedoms guaranteed under the *European Convention on Human Rights*; to make provision with respect to holders of certain judicial offices who become judges of the *European Court of Human Rights*; and for connected purposes'.

Section 1(a) of the *Human Rights Act 1998* states: 'In this Act "the Convention rights" means the rights and fundamental freedoms set out in ... Articles 2 to 12 and 14 of the Convention'. This section thereby ratifies into the United Kingdom's domestic law, and includes under its Schedules, Articles 5-7 of the ECHR, which ensures that '[e]veryone has the right to liberty and security of person' (Article 5, ECHR), 'everyone is entitled to a fair and public hearing' (Article 6, ECHR) and those convicted will not have 'a heavier penalty ... imposed than the one that was applicable at the time the criminal offence was committed' (Article 7, ECHR). These articles cover acceptable and unacceptable categories of detention and procedure.

Section 29(2)(d) of the *Scotland Act* 1998, which established the devolved Scottish Parliament, also constrains the powers of that Parliament by inhibiting it from acting in a manner incompatible with the *European Convention on Human Rights*.

The Scottish scheme avoids some of the difficulties associated with the Washington and Queensland schemes because it comes into play at the time of sentencing, eliminating the retrospectivity problem and the double punishment problem.

Conclusion

The Queensland and Washington schemes emphasise the protection of the public from sex offenders as the paramount objective. These schemes emphasise that sexually 'deviant' conduct is still intentional conduct (Morse 2003, p 167). There are a number of key differences between the Queensland and Washington schemes on the one hand and the Scottish scheme on the other. Both the Queensland and Washington schemes come into play after an offender has served his or her sentence and the Queensland scheme allows detention in a prison for the pure purpose of control (Keyzer, 2009b). The Scottish scheme is prospective (the OLR is imposed at the time of sentencing), overcoming Justice Kirby's criticism of the Queensland scheme in *Fardon v Attorney-General (Qld)*. There have been no criticisms of the Scottish regime on the basis that it inflicts double punishment or arbitrary detention.

The Scottish scheme depends on a risk assessment process coordinated by a distinct statutory body (as opposed to Corrective Services). This removes the potential for a conflict of interest that a mental health professional may experience in correctional settings, namely is the practitioner there for the prisoner or the prison? (McGuire, 2008). The Scottish scheme involves independent, fully qualified and accredited professionals, whereas, as we shall see in the next chapter, questions can be raised about the qualifications of many psychologists working in Queensland's Corrective Services (Keyzer and Coyle, 2009). Treatment is the Scottish scheme's central objective (in contrast, the Queensland scheme offers no special and related provisions to ensure adequate and appropriate rehabilitative services or resources will be made available) (Edgley, 2007). The Scottish scheme is not restricted to serious sex offenders, but enables the treatment of all high risk offenders (McFadyen, 2008).

While the United States and Queensland post-sentence preventive detention regimes have been deemed constitutional, preventive detention in punitive environments challenges long-established and widely accepted human rights principles. There are significant and unresolved human rights issues raised by the use of imprisonment to detain individuals after their criminal sentence has expired. The Scottish scheme of orders for lifelong restriction bypasses these human rights concerns by being put in place at the time of sentencing.

CHAPTER 4

Practical Issues

The preventive detention schemes in Queensland, Washington and Scotland have not been implemented without difficulties and criticisms. In this chapter we consider a number of the issues that have arisen in the course of the implementation of these schemes. Because the Scottish scheme is in the early stages of development, we focus predominantly on the Queensland model as many of the issues raised by its implementation echo those raised by the post-sentence sexually violent predator laws in the United States.

In the next chapter, we offer suggestions for reform and further research.

Queensland

Queensland has adopted a reimprisonment model for the 'care, control and treatment' of serious sex offenders (DPSOA, s 3). The DPSOA was supported by an overwhelming majority of members in the Queensland Parliament. Ninety-eight of 99 members voted in favour of the legislation, with one member abstaining on the ground that he had insufficient time to review the legislation. The DPSOA became law within 72 hours of its introduction into Parliament. As the Queensland Parliament is unicameral, there was no opportunity for further review. The legislation was not circulated for public consultation or stakeholder input (Pereira, 2003).

As a consequence of its rushed conception and introduction, the government departments charged with the responsibility of administering the legislation were poorly prepared. A significant new responsibility was added to the Attorney-General's Department, Queensland Corrective Services, Legal Aid Queensland and the Supreme Court (along with the Court of Appeal). While this is only a rough estimate (David Shepherd (2005) has noted that not all applications have resulted in published judgments), the DPSOA jurisdiction seems to account for a substantial part of the jurisdiction of the Supreme Court – 25 of the 329 decisions of the Supreme Court reported by the Australasian Legal Information Institute in 2008 were DPSOA matters (7.6 per cent).

The strain on the departments administering the DPSOA is demonstrated in the case law. In the early days of the legislation, applications by Crown Law, the Attorney-General's representative in DPSOA cases, were rushed and last minute, and consequently rejected by the Supreme Court on the ground of procedural unfairness to the accused (*Watego* (2003) 142 A Crim R 537; *Nash* (2003) 143 A Crim R 312).

There have also been problems caused by the involvement of two different government departments, that of Crown Law for the Attorney-General, and the Department of Corrective Services in the implementation of the Queensland scheme. Representatives of Crown Law have been unable to answer questions from Supreme Court justices about the need for effective resourcing of services and management of offenders in prison and under supervision in the community. These were matters for the Department of Corrective Services. This issue is considered in more detail later in this chapter. As Justice Margaret White observed in *Van Dessel* [2006] QSC 16 at [70]-[72]:

> *Some difficulties*
> When the Attorney-General commended the Bill for the [DPSOA] to the Legislative Assembly on 3 June 2003 he referred in broad terms to supervision orders but made no reference to any detail as to how they might be worked out. The [DPSOA] involves two departments of government – that of the Attorney-General who applies for an order and the Department of Corrective Services whose officers are required by s 16 to implement the supervision orders …
>
> Applications under the [DPSOA] are being made to this court regularly. Release under supervision, if it is to meet both objects of the [DPSOA], will have significant resource implications. The evidence of the psychiatrists about the continuing and specialised nature of the prisoner's rehabilitation, care or treatment when released and its limited availability suggests that officers of both the Attorney-General and the Department of Corrective Services need to address these matters in a pragmatic fashion. Justice Mackenzie referred to some similar concerns at the conclusion of his judgment in *Francis*.
>
> Some kind of temporary accommodation facility for the class of prisoner covered by the [DPSOA] whilst setting up support groups

> and employment after release or staged release might be something to consider.

Six years later, government departments are still struggling to cope with the challenges of managing serious sex offenders in Queensland.

The DPSOA and Treatment Issues

There are too few cases available and an insufficient amount of time has elapsed since the commencement of the Queensland scheme to enable the formation of firm conclusions about whether the DPSOA has led to any positive therapeutic outcomes. In addition, it is unclear why certain sex offenders have been identified as being suitable candidates for orders and others not (Douglas, 2008). Any study of the impact of the scheme in reducing recidivism would need to take that information into account. A longitudinal study will also be necessary.

It is, however, possible to glean some trends from the case law. In many cases, the Supreme Court of Queensland has ordered continuing detention on the assumption and with the hope that participation in a sex offender treatment program in prison may lead to a reduction in the risk of reoffending (see for example *B* [2006] QSC 227 at [53]; *Beattie* [2007] QCA 96; *Fisher* [2007] QSC 212, [2007] QSC 341 at [27]; *Bridson* [2007] QSC 307 at [55]; *Hynds* [2007] QSC 374; *Shapland* [2007] QSC 344 (following *B*); *WW* [2007] QCA 334; *Yeo* [2006] QSC 63, [2008] QCA 115 at [12]-[13]; *Carpenter* [2008] QSC 225 at [22]; *Winston* [2009] QSC 11). In *Waghorn* [2006] QSC 171 at [20] Justice Margaret McMurdo pointed out that 'at present the absence of a successful completion of the program substantially affects the risk of offending'.

In some of the periodic review cases, after a prisoner has participated in such a program, the court has concluded that the risk the prisoner poses to the community has decreased, justifying a supervision order rather than continuing detention (see for example *Banks* [2007] QSC 267; *Harvey* [2007] QSC 366; *Levack* [2007] QSC 275 at [77]; *Deverill* [2008] QSC 5; *Hancock* [2008] QSC 338; and *Currie* [2009] QSC 112 at [9]).

However, failure to complete a sex offender treatment program has not always been regarded as an impediment to release (see for example *B* [2006] QSC 227; *Spence* [2007] QSC 218; *Yeo* [2007] QSC 274; *Bryde* [2008] QSC 94 at [13], [18]; *Hancock* [2008] QSC 338; *Voois* [2008] QSC 168). In some cases, judges have held that sex offender treatment programs may not serve any purpose when a person has not been diagnosed with a paraphilia (*Fardon* [2006] QSC 275 at [65]; *Shapland* [2007] QSC 344). In addition, courts have accepted psychiatric evidence that prison-based sex offender treatment programs may not have reduced the risk below 'high' that a prisoner may commit another serious sexual offence (*Friend* [2008] QSC 27 at [23]; *Levack* [2007] QSC 275 at [77]; *LSS* [2007] QSC 202 at [18], [22]; *Robinson* [2006] QSC 328 and [2007] QCA 111; *Wright* [2006] QSC 389; *Fisher* [2007] QSC 341; *Twigge* [2006] QSC 107; *Van Dessel* [2006] QCA 285; and *Currie* [2009] QSC 112 at [9]).

One question that requires further research and consideration is the question whether the sex offender treatment programs operating in Queensland prisons, which serious sex offenders are compelled to attend under the DPSOA, actually reduce reoffending. Marion Lees (2001) has reported positive outcomes with the Queensland Indigenous Sex Offenders Program. But Robert Schweitzer and Jonathan Dwyer (2003) have suggested that there has been no statistically significant reduction in recidivism following participation in Queensland's prison-based sexual offender treatment programs. Schweitzer and Dwyer conclude that the initial promise of sexual offender treatment programs must be further examined by individual and meta-analytic studies.

In the absence of evidence that prisons should be a venue for treatment, legitimate questions can be raised about whether reimprisonment serves any purpose other than the further control of the offenders (Keyzer, 2009b). Reimprisonment for the sole purpose of control raises the spectre of double punishment which we considered in Chapter 3. As Robert Hayes and his co-authors (2009) have observed:

> If treatment for sex offenders did lower the risk of future offending, this argument would be very persuasive as most of the offenders brought before the courts in New South Wales and Queensland have refused to participate in prison-based treatment programmes. However, despite published outcome studies describing as many as 20,000 offenders who have completed custody-based group therapy treatment programmes worldwide, there is very little evidence that psychological treatments in custody reduces the risk of sexual recidivism (referring to Kenworthy et al, 2007).

Indeed, it appears that the majority of properly controlled (international) studies of the effectiveness of sexual offender treatment programs conducted in correctional facilities have failed to yield positive results (Hanson and Bussiere, 2002; Seager et al, 2004; Marques et al, 2005). There is some evidence that some interventions can increase the likelihood of recidivism in the long term (Hayes et al, 2009), but the evidence available on treatment program effectiveness has led Robert Hayes and his co-authors to conclude:

> Until custody-based treatment programmes are shown to be effective we can only conclude that the need to provide treatment to reduce the risk of recidivism is poor justification for preventative detention.

In positing the question 'do Queensland's sex offender treatment programs work?' it is not suggested that sex offender treatment programs in Queensland prisons should be abandoned because the evidence of their effectiveness is marginal. As Denise Lievore (2004, p 102) and John La Fond (2005, p 57) have observed, given the extremely negative impact of sexual offending on victims and their families, even small reductions in recidivism are of great value. The sensible course is to provide the best possible services and to conduct research into their impact.

There is some recent research supporting the use of community-based, sex offender treatment programs, where there is ongoing involvement with an offender, by highly trained professionals, whilst they are in the community (Gelb, 2007; Wilson and Wales, 2008; Hanson, Harris, Scott and Helmus, 2007). This suggests that continued preventive detention in prison for the purpose of treatment might not be the best option.

At present there are some reasons to be pessimistic about the prospect of effective sex offender treatment being given within a corrective facility in Queensland (Keyzer and Coyle, 2009). First, sex offender treatment programs are only made available to a limited number of prisoners even though they are practically compelled to attend by the DPSOA (*McLean* [2006] QSC 137). Second, offenders must wait long periods of time before they have an opportunity to participate in a sex offender treatment program (see for example, *Twigge* [2006] QSC 107 at [13]-[14] and *W* [2004] QSC 262 at [4]). The facts of *Gough v Southern Queensland Regional Parole Board* [2008] QSC 222 illustrate this problem. In this case, sex offender James Gough, representing himself, brought an application in the Supreme Court for judicial review of a decision by the Parole Board to deny him parole. Gough had been sentenced on 24 November 2006 to four-and-a-half years' imprisonment and was given a parole eligibility date of 24 February 2008. On 25 October 2007 the Parole Board received an application for parole from Gough, who indicated that he had 'continually and persistently lobbied prison authorities to be permitted to participate in appropriate intervention courses' but his pleas had 'fallen on deaf ears' (at [2]). Justice Peter Applegarth observed at [6]:

> For reasons that are unexplained by the evidence, Queensland Corrective Services did not offer the applicant one of the intervention programs that the applicant was prepared to undertake so as to enable him to commence, let alone complete, the programs prior to his application for parole being considered in late 2007 and prior to his parole eligibility date of 24 February 2008. In the result, the applicant, through no fault of his own, was unable to rely in his application to the Board upon the results of his participation in such programs. The relapse prevention plan that the applicant submitted was not enhanced by any benefits that such programs may have provided to him.

Justice Applegarth noted that Queensland Corrective Services had provided no evidence to the court that it was not practicable for the prisoner to enter and complete the recommended programs prior to his parole eligibility date (at [57]). Yet the Parole Board had stated in its reasons for denying parole that Gough lacked insight regarding his pattern of offending behaviour and that this 'was to be expected, *given that he had not completed any interventions*' (emphasis added) (at [61]). Justice Applegarth concluded that the Parole Board erred in law by reaching its conclusion to deny parole without any regard to why the applicant had yet to complete the programs (at [72]).

Assuming that participation in a treatment program is seen as a beneficial activity – and the courts certainly seem to be operating on that assumption in DPSOA cases – failure to participate by reason of administrative oversight can hardly be seen as conducive to effective rehabilitation and community safety (see also *Perkins* [2009] QSC 53 at [53]-[54]).

Another significant problem with sex offender treatment programs in Queensland prisons is that they are not available in every prison (Catholic Prison Ministry and Prisoners Legal Service, 2008, p 31). This means that prisoners in rural and regional Queensland must move to a different prison in order to participate (see for example *Bridson* [2007]

QSC 307 at [52]). It can be acknowledged that sex offender treatment programs require the involvement of qualified personnel and may be resource intensive. It may therefore be considered impracticable or too expensive to run a sex offender treatment program in every prison in Queensland. However, it must also be acknowledged that moving a prisoner can break up the often fragile community ties that a prisoner may have retained or developed with a local community during his or her prison term (*McLean* [2006] QSC 137 at [13]; *Bridson* [2007] QSC 307 at [52]). Breaking up these community ties – particularly arrangements that yield the prospect of a workable accommodation placement after release – can increase the stress on a prisoner when and if he or she is released, enhancing the risk of reoffending. Given the at best equivocal evidence regarding the success of prison-based sex offender treatment programs, and the comparatively strong evidence that appropriate post-prison accommodation arrangements reduce reoffending (considered below), there is a strong case for bringing the treatment to the prisoner rather than vice versa.

Other problems have emerged from the protocols adopted by Queensland Corrective Services when processing prisoners for the purpose of placement in sex offender treatment programs. It appears that a sex offender who is serving time for manslaughter is deemed ineligible for a sex offender treatment program (*Sutherland* [2006] QSC 268). Some individuals with intellectual disabilities are deemed ineligible for sex offender treatment programs because it is assumed that they will fail to understand what is going on (*B* [2006] QSC 227). While there may be individual extenuating circumstances justifying a decision not to place a person in a treatment program, surely all efforts should be made to include offenders, rather than to exclude them, from sex offender treatment programs.

One aspect of the program placement process operating in Queensland seems particularly odd. It appears that it is standard practice to reclassify prisoners who have been returned to prison via the DPSOA to a high security classification, even though they may have been on a low or 'open' classification beforehand (*Banks* [2007] QSC 267 and *Kondos* [2008] QSC 295). In *Fardon* [2006] QCA 512 at [18], the President of the Court of Appeal, Justice Margaret McMurdo, noted that this reclassification occurred 'despite the respondent's lengthy period of good behaviour … and through no fault of his own'.

The consequence for Fardon was that he would not be eligible for graduated release.

The reclassification practice has rendered other offenders ineligible to attend a sex offender treatment program, which is, of course, precisely the reason for which they were reimprisoned (*Gough v Parole Board* [2008] QSC 222 and *McLean* [2006] QSC 137 at [14]). Referring to the observations made by the Court of Appeal in *Francis*, which were critical of Corrective Services for their failure to effect a management plan for that prisoner, Justice Glen Williams wrote in *Fardon* [2006] QCA 512 at [32]-[33]:

> That change in his classification was brought about despite any conduct on the part of the respondent which would have justified reclassifying him. One can readily understand the frustrations that the respondent must feel, particularly when impartial observers might reasonably conclude that Corrective Services was frustrating any real attempt to provide for the gradual release referred to by all examining psychiatrists. That sort of frustration is only likely to exacerbate the respondent's condition and in the long run make it more difficult for him to rehabilitate himself in society.
>
> As it now seems clear that Corrective Services are unable, or unwilling, to provide the gradual release procedure recommended by all examining psychiatrists, the time has come, particularly given the observations of the Court of Appeal in *A-G (Qld) v Francis* [2006] QCA 324, to approve his release on the conditions proposed by the learned judge at first instance.

It is unclear why sex offenders should be reclassified after they are made subject to orders under the DPSOA. If a prisoner has a lengthy period of good conduct, then it seems arbitrary to change his or her classification by reference to the risk he or she may pose to the community if released. If this type of reclassification removes the prisoner from eligibility for programs, this is plainly a retrograde step.

Treatment programs may also be needed to address issues of substance abuse. Many of the offenders reimprisoned under the DPSOA have been substance abusers, and substance abuse has been a factor in their offending (see for example *B* [2006] QSC 227; *Bickle* [2006] QSC 130; *Bridson* [2007] QSC 307; *Edwards* [2007] QSC 396; *Fardon* [2006] QSC 275 at [16]; *Fisher* [2007] QSC 341 at [41]; *Foy* [2007] QSC 141; *Francis* [2007] QSC 367; *Hansen* [2006] QSC 35; *HTR* [2007] QSC 19; *Levack* [2007] QSC 275; *McLean* [2006] QSC 137; *O'Rourke* [2006] QSC 196; *Robinson* [2007] QCA 111; *Smith* [2008] QSC 22; *Sutherland* [2006]

QSC 268; *Toms* [2006] QSC 298; *Twigge* [2006] QSC 107; *Van Dessel* [2006] QSC 16; *Watego* [2003] QSC 367; *Yeo* [2006] QSC 63 at [10]; *Currie* [2009] QSC 112 at [11]; *Wilson* [2009] QSC 36; *George* [2009] QSC 2 at [19]; *Hancock* [2008] QSC 338; *Burke* [2008] QSC 313; *Sambo* [2008] QSC 262; and *Carpenter* [2008] QSC 225 at [13]). Substance abuse is a recognised risk factor in many sexual assault cases (Hayes et al, 2009). The effective rehabilitation of sex offenders with substance abuse problems must include services designed to minimise the prospect of substance abuse upon release. However while substance abuse programs are run more frequently in Queensland prisons than sex offender treatment programs, they are also not run regularly in every prison in Queensland. Relapse prevention programs should be made available for people on supervision orders under the DPSOA.

The Risk Assessment Process

Currently, section 9 of the DPSOA requires reports on the offender's risk from two psychiatrists. As outlined in Chapter 2, this has been criticised as discriminating against forensic psychologists who use actuarial risk assessment scales (Mercado and Ogloff, 2006). In a 2008 report, Queensland Corrective Services recommended that their personnel should have a greater role in the risk assessment process (Queensland Corrective Services, 2008, pp 13-14). Specifically, it was recommended that the DPSOA should be 'amended to mandate that the court consider in addition to any risk assessment provided, a report from Queensland Corrective Services as to an offender's suitability for release into the community at the time of making an initial order, upon review or for the purposes of any breach proceedings' (Queensland Corrective Services, 2008, p 14). Leaving aside the constitutional difficulties that may accompany 'mandating' the court's consideration of any type of evidence (*Chu Kheng Lim v Minister for Immigration* (1992) 176 CLR 1 at 37), there may be other problems associated with having Queensland Corrective Services personnel conducting final risk assessments, given both their level of qualifications and lack of independence (Keyzer and Coyle, 2009). These recommendations have not been included in the Dangerous Prisoners (Sexual Offenders) and Other Legislation Amendment Bill 2009.

Apparently, many of the psychologists employed within Queensland Corrective Services are interns (Keyzer and Coyle, 2009).

As far as can be ascertained, there are very few psychologists employed within Queensland Corrective Services who are fully qualified forensic psychologists. Given the significance of the evidence of prison officials in the offender identification and management process, explained in previous chapters, this is plainly a significant issue. Further, the tests presently used by Queensland Corrective Services to determine the risk of recidivism have been criticised as not providing adequate predictions of any particular individual's propensity to reoffend (Coyle, 2008). In fact, as explored in Chapter 2, it has been argued that the results of these tests are problematic in predicting whether a particular individual will reoffend (Hart et al, 2007). Although there are tests that include both static and dynamic risk factors and that are claimed to have a high diagnostic accuracy, the administration of these tests and the assessment of the results require a high level of skill and experience.

On at least one occasion the Supreme Court has been critical of the quality of some of the expert evidence led in DPSOA cases (see *Toms* [2006] QSC 298 at [35]-[38]). As we noted in Chapter 2, Scotland has an independent agency, the Risk Management Authority, that accredits risk assessors and sets out standards for risk assessments. There is a compelling case for an independent body to be charged with the responsibility of conducting risk assessments in Queensland, as takes place in Scotland. As James McGuire (2008, p 112) has observed:

> In correctional settings ... [ethical] dilemmas turn upon a question of what is the basic purpose of a psychologist's work, and who is the client. Is the psychologist there primarily to address the needs of the individual who has broken (or might break) the law, and to provide counselling, therapy or other services that will promote and sustain psychological well-being? Alternatively, is the pre-eminent objective to protect society, to serve an employer (possibly the state), to assess and manage risk?

A system that enables independent, accredited mental health professionals to conduct risk assessments – like the Risk Management Authority in Scotland – is preferable. It avoids the ethical dilemma identified by McGuire. The development of an independent authority that vets the professional qualifications of its experts would also help to ensure that risk assessments satisfy minimum standards of quality and rigour. We return to this proposal in the concluding chapter.

Applications under the DPSOA

As we noted in Chapter 1, the Serious Sexual Offenders Review Committee identifies and processes prisoners under the DPSOA. The Committee meets monthly to review eligible prisoners and obtain legal advice from Crown Law as to the prospects of success of an application under the Act. The review occurs when the prisoner is 18 months from full time discharge (this obviously did not take place until the legislation was 18 months old, in early 2005). The Crown Solicitor then makes a recommendation to the Attorney-General who decides whether to proceed with an application. Prisoners are eligible for consideration for orders under the DPSOA if they are in custody and serving a sentence of more than two years' imprisonment that includes a period for a serious sexual offence. A person who has committed only one offence can be the subject of an order under the DPSOA (*Gadd* [2008] QSC 247).

In Chapter 3 we noted the difficulties that affected a number of the early applications under the Act, in particular, delay in advancing applications until the final weeks or even days before the expiry of the prisoner's sentence. In some cases this was a factor in the Supreme Court concluding that there had been a denial of natural justice (*Watego* (2003) 142 A Crim R 537; *Nash* (2003) 143 A Crim R 312). Supreme Court judges have criticised the practice of late applications, which inconveniences the court and increases the pressure on (typically less well-funded) defence counsel (see for example *Foy* [2004] QSC 428). The court has upheld applications made only a month before the conclusion of a person's sentence (*Francis* [2004] QSC 128) - but not without criticism. In *Francis*, Justice Kenneth Mackenzie observed at [6]:

> The problem caused by late applications is that a respondent is likely to spend some months beyond the date of completion of his sentence before a final determination is made. A fairer balance might be achieved if there was a requirement to bring the application no earlier than six months before the prisoner's release date and no later than three months before that date. That would require an amendment to the law, but would at least allow more time for preparation of the independent reports of the two psychiatrists named by the court pursuant to s 8(2)(a) and any reports or evidence upon which a prisoner wishes to rely and to conduct a final hearing close to the prisoner's release date if not before. Apart from the possibility that some administrative effort would

> be wasted if an application was ultimately not made, it would promote a more timely disposition of matters if identification of material relevant to the application was carried out concurrently with any psychiatric evaluation. One would hope that the risk of wasted effort could be minimised by selecting cases where an application was to be considered with sufficient discrimination to limit the possibility that the statutory criteria would not be met upon closer examination.

Similar comments have been made in other cases (see for example the comments in *W* [2004] QSC 262 at [15]).

Annual Reviews

After an initial wave of applications for continuing detention orders in late 2003 and 2004, review hearings for reincarcerated prisoners started to come before the Queensland courts in late 2004 and early 2005. Part 3 of the DPSOA, which is entitled 'Annual reviews', authorises periodic reviews of prisoners who have been reincarcerated under the regime. Periodic review would appear to satisfy the international human rights requirements identified by the majority in the United Nations Human Rights Committee's decision in *Rameka v New Zealand* (No 1090/2002, 15 December 2003), subject to our other observations in Chapter 3.

Unsurprisingly, successful completion of a sex offender treatment program will ordinarily yield a favourable annual review (*Kondos* [2008] QSC 295). This is certainly the case where the risk is judged to have been reduced (*Little* [2008] QSC 269). But, as we noted above, supervision orders can and often are made where the prisoner is still judged to be at high risk of reoffending (see for example *Bridson* [2008] QSC 281).

However, it appears that 'annual reviews' under the DPSOA do not actually result in a prisoner being reviewed annually. The annual review provisions of the DPSOA only require that applications by the Attorney-General to continue the detention of prisoners beyond the conclusion of their previous detention orders must take place within one year of the last order of the court (*Fardon* [2006] QSC 5). In other words, if a person is subjected to a continuing detention order on 1 January 2007, it is not necessary for the Attorney-General to make an application in sufficient time for a further review to be completed by 1 January 2008; it is only necessary for the Attorney-General's application to be lodged within a year of the previous order. In practical terms, this means that a person subject to the DPSOA is reimprisoned for periods of more like 18 months at a time, rather than 12 months (Keyzer and O'Toole, 2006).

Taking into account the fact that a continuing detention order tends to last 18 rather than 12 months, the recent recommendation of Queensland Corrective Services (2008) to lengthen continuing detention orders from 'one' to two years is very likely to mean that they will last two-and-a-half years (Keyzer and Coyle, 2009). The Queensland Corrective Services report (2008, p 24), recommending the extension of preventive imprisonment orders, describes the rationale for that step in the following terms:

> The annual review of continuing detention orders currently creates considerable difficulties for QCS in terms of its ability to obtain up-to-date evidence for the purpose of these reviews. A longer period between reviews would allow for an application to be made on the best available evidence as to the offender's current risk status. This would give QCS sufficient time to implement the Court's recommendations and assess the offender's progress in achieving the goals in his IMP. More importantly it would allow offenders sufficient time to demonstrate a change in behaviour and reduction in risk and for offenders to engage in the intensive sexual offender rehabilitation programs and consolidate treatment gains. For these reasons the IWG proposes that the period between legislated reviews of continuing detention orders be increased to two years.

It is very difficult to understand why Queensland Corrective Services should need a period of two years to administer a sex offender treatment program and conduct a review of an offender's progress when none of the programs presently offered in Queensland prisons lasts longer than about 40 weeks (and this program is made up of only a few meetings per week). It is especially difficult to understand why two years is needed for the purposes outlined above when the committee that has the task of referring offenders to the Attorney-General for consideration (whether an application should be filed with the Supreme Court to keep them in prison) meets to consider the suitability of offenders for orders under the DPSOA some 18 months before that offender's sentence is due to end. Given the very serious incursion on civil liberty that a continuing detention order represents, administrative convenience should not be a factor in calibrating the length of continuing detention orders.

It would be sensible, and consistent with the principles of procedural fairness, if the Serious Sexual Offenders Review Committee could also notify offenders of the decision to refer their case to the Attorney-General when that occurs. Offenders could then work with Queensland Corrective Services to help get access to a treatment program before their sentence expires (Keyzer and Coyle, 2009). This might even remove the need for an application to be made under the DPSOA, lessening the workload for all government departments concerned and, incidentally, allowing prisoners to be released at the conclusion of their prison terms. As we noted above, offenders have been denied parole or judged to be a high risk to the community because they have not completed a sexual offender treatment program through no fault of their own.

A final general comment should be made about the DPSOA application process. Prisoners are often poor, and virtually all of them rely on representation by Legal Aid. While this representation is of the highest standard, prisoners are rarely in a position to fund the appointment of an expert witness or witnesses to analyse the reports prepared by the court-appointed psychiatrist for the purpose of a DPSOA hearing. Yet the involvement of an expert witness coming from a critical perspective may be vital to exposing deficiencies in the evidence (see for example *Nash* (2003) 143 A Crim R 312 at 314; *Fardon* [2005] QSC 137 at [18]). An independent and realistic analysis of the relative resourcing of the legal agencies prosecuting and defending DPSOA applications should be conducted to ensure that all the lawyers who are working in this jurisdiction have adequate resources to do their job.

The Failure to Provide Treatment

In the course of the annual review cases, the Supreme Court and Court of Appeal have noted the problems that Queensland Corrective Services have had in managing offenders reincarcerated under the DPSOA (Keyzer and O'Toole, 2006). In *Francis* [2005] QSC 381, Justice Kenneth Mackenzie was plainly concerned by the failure of Queensland Corrective Services to implement a plan ordered by the Supreme Court for the treatment of Darren Francis, remarking that 'if there isn't a government commitment to facilitate the plan, then it is a question whether I should order [Darren Francis'] continuing detention to give effect to it'. Justice Mackenzie continued at [33]:

> It cannot be lost sight of that the [DPSOA] is concerned with preventative detention after the prisoner would otherwise have been released by effluxion of his finite sentence. Undue protraction of incarceration of the person because administrative procedures either do not exist to enable him to rehabilitate sufficiently to be released, or to prove that the actual risk in his case is not unacceptable, or because the administrative procedures unduly delay such rehabilitation or proof, is hard to convincingly justify. The [DPSOA] is, after all, intended by its terms to allow continued detention only for as long as the unacceptable risk to the community clearly exists. It is not intended to lock up people and throw away the key if they may have prospects of rehabilitation to an extent where they can be released, given the opportunity, but are denied that opportunity due to administrative or procedural inadequacies.

While more recent hearings involving Darren Francis have demonstrated a superior response on the part of Corrective Services (*Attorney-General (Qld) v Francis* [2007] QSC 328), other recent cases indicate that responses have not improved across the board (Keyzer, 2009b).

For example, *Lawrence* [2008] QSC 230 concerned a 47-year-old man with an extensive criminal history from aggravated assaults against children escalating to rape and manslaughter. Mark Lawrence received a further sentence for rape in prison, but was eligible for release in late 2008. Although Lawrence participated in a variety of programs in prison, including a sex offender treatment program, psychiatric risk assessments conducted for the purpose of his dangerous prisoners hearing concluded that he remained a high risk of committing further violent sexual offences ([2003] QSC 230 at [18]-[23]). The relevant government departments appeared to be either unwilling or unable to develop a suitable post-release service plan. Justice Henry Fryberg observed at [52]:

> [The] continued detention of Mr Lawrence is antithetical to the creation of a set of requirements for his release in circumstances where the risk to the community would be acceptable. From the therapeutic point of view the risk to the community cannot be reduced by his continued detention. Indeed such detention places at risk the gains which have been made until now.

Instead Justice Fryberg concluded that what Mark Lawrence needed was a gradual and closely supervised release into the community, accommodation, employment and access to one-on-one counselling along with (initially) 24-hour support (at [46]-[53]). Ironically, such a program may have been possible before the Queensland Parliament enacted the *Corrective Services Act 2006*, but that Act abolished such programs (at [53]). According to Justice Fryberg, such a system may well have satisfied the therapeutic objectives outlined by the expert witnesses that Lawrence's risk could be managed in the community.

Justice Fryberg then addressed the limitations on the Queensland Department of Corrective Services' capacity to play its part in monitoring people released under supervision orders at [57]-[58]:

> To implement supervision orders the Government has established the Sexual Offender Dangerous Offender Unit within the Department of Corrective Services. The purpose of the unit is to oversee the supervision and surveillance of offenders released on supervision orders, with the focus on community protection and reducing reoffending. This involves ensuring that appropriate case management processes are undertaken by staff to ensure offenders comply with the requirements of this supervision. The Acting Director of that unit, Mr Smith, described that process as an operational approach to tailoring responses to the individual needs of the offender. He testified that tailoring the management to the individual was one of the main concepts of the process. In March 2008 he estimated that there were about 40 persons subject to supervision orders and six to eight in continuing detention.
>
> Qualitatively the SODO unit is capable of providing 24-hour supervision of the sort just described. It can do this not only by providing personnel, but also by electronic monitoring, the enforcement of curfew restrictions, random testing for alcohol and drugs and use of closed-circuit television. *However it is not presently funded by the Treasury to do so* (emphasis added).

(It may be noted that that the unit was set up in June 2007 and material relating to its functions was published on the Queensland Corrective Services website in October 2007.) In light of the absence of suitable facilities for Mark Lawrence's staged release, and the risk associated with making a supervision order in light of the fact that the Sexual Offender Dangerous Offenders Unit was not then funded to do its job properly, Justice Fryberg concluded that he could not make a supervision order (at [69]). Accordingly, Justice Fryberg made a continuing detention order (at [72]). Since there was no therapeutic reason to keep Lawrence in prison, this order could only be made for the purposes of control.

Challenging the government's unwillingness or inability to build a suitable transition arrangement for Lawrence, Justice Fryberg said that the 'evidence before me does not suggest that it would be impractical or unreasonable for the Government to make suitable facilities available for housing Lawrence (if they are needed and do not already exist), at least after a year from now. The Government has a positive obligation to implement the preventive objects of the Act' (at [71]). Citing the Court of Appeal judgment in *Francis* [2007] 1 Qd R 396 at 401-402 (as noted in Chapter 3), Justice Fryberg repeated the court's comment:

> It is possible, too, that the view taken by Gummow J in *Fardon v Attorney-General for Queensland* supports an argument that executive government repudiation of the preventive objects of the [DPSOA] in a particular case (as, for example, by the refusal of any treatment to a prisoner clearly capable of, and amenable to, rehabilitation) could lead the court to refuse to make any order at all. If it were to appear to the court that any further detention would be truly punitive in character and, thus, contrary to the intention of the legislation, there would be no basis for the court to make an order of any kind under the [DPSOA]. The conditions of further restraint upon the detainee's liberty would be out of character with the intention of the legislature: that such restraint is preventive. The character of the detention authorised by the [DPSOA] is, as was explained in the reasons of the High Court in *Fardon v Attorney-General for Queensland*, not punitive but preventive.

Justice Fryberg concluded that 'an unreasonable failure to provide suitable facilities might constitute another example' (at [71]).

Mark Lawrence appealed to the Court of Appeal, seeking a supervision order to replace his continuing detention order. The Court of Appeal rejected the appeal (*Lawrence* [2009] QCA 136). The Court held that the objects clause of the DPSOA contemplates three *alternative* purposes: care *or* control *or* treatment (see also *Francis* [2007] 1 Qd R 396 at 401). The Court of Appeal rejected the argument that Lawrence's imprisonment for the purpose of control was effectively punitive because he had not been given any treatment. As Justice Peter Applegarth observed in *Sambo* [2008] QSC 262 at [100]: 'Any ineptitude or maladministration by the department [of Corrective Services] in not placing the respondent on a program at an earlier time is of no real consequence so far as it affects the task of the Court under the Act'.

Supervision Orders under the DPSOA

As we noted in Chapter 3, in *Francis* [2006] QCA 324 at [39] the Court of Appeal held:

> If supervision of the prisoner is apt to ensure adequate protection, having regard to the risk to the community posed by the prisoner, then an order for supervised release should, in principle, be preferred to a continuing detention order on the basis that the intrusions of the [DPSOA] upon the liberty of the subject are exceptional, and the liberty of the subject should be constrained to no greater extent than is warranted by the statute which authorized such constraint.

Accordingly, the majority of orders made under the DPSOA are supervision orders, which certainly contrasts with the operation of the United States 'inpatient' regimes, where very few offenders have ever been released (La Fond, 2005, p 149). There has been only one case in which a continuing detention order or supervision order has been refused on merit (*W* no judgment published – the preliminary hearing judgment is published as *W* [2004] QSC 262). The Attorney-General bears the onus of demonstrating that the risk of reoffending remains unacceptable if the prisoner is released under supervision (*Francis* [2006] QCA 324; *Waghorn* [2006] QSC 171; *Hynds* [2007] QSC 374; *Taylor* [2008] QSC 183). A number of Supreme Court decisions demonstrate awareness of this and supervision orders have been crafted to respond to the risk factors that seem relevant to the individual offender (*Yeo* [2008] QCA 115 at [48]; *Bickle* [2008] QSC 211 at [16]).

As with the question of the therapeutic benefits of preventive detention, it is impossible to draw firm conclusions about whether the supervision order regime is working. However, in *Murry* [2007] QSC 121, Justice Richard Chesterman accepted a submission by counsel for the Attorney-General that few offenders had then breached their supervision orders and remarked at [6]:

> One hears, sometimes, and from some quarters, a suggestion that prisoners jailed for committing sexual offences, especially against children, should never be released. The figures I was given do not support such a position. Only one in six (almost) of those released has not complied with the conditions imposed. Keeping six men

> in jail indefinitely after they have served their sentence, thereby destroying their lives, scarcely seems justified if only one of them might re-offend if released. The figures suggest that supervision orders are effective to prevent recidivism.

One additional problem that has emerged is that many prisoners have an intellectual disability or some other cognitive impairment (often caused by substance abuse or by virtue of an acquired brain injury) that makes it difficult for them to understand instructions (*B* [2006] QSC 227; *Bryde* [2008] QSC 94 at [7]; *Downs* [2005] QSC 16, [2008] QSC 87 at [4]; *Fisher* [2007] QSC 341 at [34]; *Foy* [2005] QSC 1 at [17]; *LSS* [2007] QSC 202 at [31]; *Winston* [2009] QSC 11). Queensland Corrective Services now offers these prisoners sex offender treatment programs (*Winston* [2009] QSC 11), but it is unclear whether all are offered access (*B* [2006] QSC 227). In addition, the typical supervision order has 30 or 40 detailed provisions, which can make compliance difficult. In *Fisher* [2007] QSC 341 at [34]-[35] Justice Kenneth Mackenzie stated:

> There was a general observation that, given the intellectual limitations of the respondent, the form of order should be as simple as possible. I do not disagree with that notion but there is a difficulty in drafting in basic English. It tends to risk a lack of precision in stating what are, to most who are familiar with the law, well known concepts. Further, some of the provisions mirror the terms of the legislation and should not be departed from without good reason.
>
> While orders have to be tailored to individual cases, where particular requirements have become common to many orders, it is probably counterproductive to express them differently, in case it be thought that there is a distinction between the obligations in individual cases. I was advised from the Bar table that the requirements of the order are, in practice, fully explained by an authorised Corrections Officer so that the person subject to the order is fully aware of what the obligations are. If a prisoner is functionally or substantially illiterate, that is the only way in which he can be adequately informed of the nature of the restrictions to which he will be subject …

While unavoidable, this approach plainly reinforces a power imbalance between supervisory personnel and the offender (Alexander, 2009).

Supervision Order Breaches

Typically any breach of a supervision order is the subject of an application to the Supreme Court (DPSOA, ss 20-22). A constitutional challenge to these provisions on grounds similar to those rejected in *Fardon v Attorney-General (Qld)* (2004) 223 CLR 575 was rejected in *Francis* (2008) 250 ALR 555 at [52] and [108]-[109].

Under section 21 of the DPSOA, the supervisee must satisfy the court on the balance of probabilities that his detention in custody pending a final determination is not justified in light of 'exceptional circumstances' (*Fisher* [2009] QSC 104). A trivial breach may constitute exceptional circumstances (*Francis* (2008) 250 ALR 555 at 581 [110]; *Fisher* [2009] QSC 104). The duration of the period until the section 22 hearing is also relevant to the assessment of risk – if the hearing is only a few weeks away, offenders are considered to have a strong incentive not to breach their conditions (*Francis* [2008] QSC 69 at [7]; adopted by the Court of Appeal in *Francis* (2008) 250 ALR 555 at 566 [41]). Occasional use of alcohol and even illegal drugs has been seen as constituting a trivial breach (*Bragg* [2009] QSC 9; *Toms* [2008] QSC 131). But the courts have been more concerned when substance abuse has been a significant factor in previous sexual offending (*Fisher* [2009] QSC 104 at [6]; *Wilson* [2009] QSC 36). Access to child pornography constituted a breach resulting in the imposition of a more stringent supervision order in *Wright* [2008] QSC 237. Leaving the jurisdiction and failing to report to a corrective services officer or to a consulting psychiatrist have been seen as major breaches justifying further detention (*O'Rourke* [2008] QSC 153).

The Supreme Court has recognised that the objective of section 22, which enables the making of further orders, is to protect the community from the risk of a serious sexual offence, rather than offences generally, and has acceded to submissions filed by counsel for supervisees that supervision orders should be trimmed to remove 'no offences' requirements and replace them with 'no sexual offences' requirements (*Deverill* [2008] QSC 5; *Thumm* [2008] QSC 180 at [9]-[13]; *Sambo* [2008] QSC 262 at [88]). In *Bryde* [2008] QSC 94 at [32], Justice Dutney explained that to commit a person to detention in prison when he was alleged to have committed an offence that was not a sexual offence was beyond the scope of the DPSOA and would 'gratuitously impose double punishment'.

Post-Release Accommodation and Services

Expert witnesses in dangerous prisoner cases often recommend that people being released from prison should have immediate access (*O'Rourke* [2008] QSC 153; contrast *Francis* [2008] QSC 69) to community-based sex offender treatment 'maintenance' programs (*Deverill* [2008] QSC 5). At present, however, there are limited sex offender treatment programs available for persons released on supervision orders (*Bridson* [2007] QSC 307 at [52]). While the Sexual Offender Maintenance Program is presently available in the Brisbane Central region, it is not yet available in Townsville or Cairns (although it was intended that it would be in early 2009) and it will not be available in Ipswich or Southport until the end of 2009 (Alexander, 2009). This is in spite of the fact that in *Beattie* [2006] QSC 322, which was decided three years ago, Justice John Helman observed:

> There are at present six programs available in custodial centres: the High Intensity Sexual Offending Program (HISOP), the Medium Intensity Sexual Offending Program (MISOP), the Indigenous High Intensity Sexual Offending Program (IHISOP), the Indigenous Medium Intensity Sexual Offending Program (IMISOP), the Sexual Offending Maintenance Program (SOMP), and the Getting Started: Preparatory Program (GS:PP). *The MISOP and the SOMP will soon be available to offenders subject to community-based orders*, but for offenders of moderate-high to high risk of re-offending who have not completed a program the HISOP is the most appropriate, but is available only in custodial centres (emphasis added).

In some cases, Queensland Corrective Services has demonstrated a willingness to meet the cost of treatment services in the community (*Twigge* [2006] QSC 107). In *Voois* [2008] QSC 168, Queensland Corrective Services offered to fund services that enabled a supervisee to undertake medical procedures. But in many other cases, judges have been disappointed with the failure of Queensland Corrective Services to develop suitable post-release service plans (Keyzer, 2009b). Because the government will not fund group therapy services in the community, Supreme Court judges are faced with the difficult choice of making a continuing detention order to ensure that a prisoner has access to such services or making a supervision order in circumstances where Queensland Corrective Services offers limited or negligible services (*Perkins* [2009] QSC 53 at [84]). At present there is limited support available to *released* sex offenders, which, adopting the 'risk-needs' paradigm of offender therapy, could only be expected to exacerbate the risk that these offenders represent to society.

Research suggests that there is a high correlation between the lack of post-release housing options and recidivism (Baldry, McDonnell, Maplestone and Peters, 2002). Unfortunately, housing options for people released from prison are extremely limited. People released from prison are typically dependent on welfare or have low incomes which, when coupled with the stigma associated with time inside, can make it very difficult to obtain private tenancies (Borzycki and Baldry, 2003). Public housing options may also be limited due to previous rent defaults. People released under supervision pursuant to the DPSOA may have even more limited options, as these orders tend to be very strict and, unsurprisingly, are zealously policed (*Toms* [2007] QSC 290). In addition, pre-release housing and community support planning tends to be ad hoc and is often inadequately resourced (Baldry et al, 2002, p 4).

It is obvious that the risk that an offender poses to the community will be heightened if the government fails to arrange or fund post-prison community-based release programs, including appropriate housing, employment and social services that make transition from prison to the community possible (see for example *Foy* [2005] QSC 1 at [6]; *Fardon* [2007] QSC 299 at [29] and [2006] QCA 512 [27]; *Toms* [2007] QSC 290 at [15]-[16]; *Yeo* [2007] QSC 274 at [42]; *Francis* [2007] QSC 367; *Downs* [2005] QSC 16; *Reynolds* [2007] QSC 52 at [28]; *Robinson* [2007] QCA 111). Instead, judges have recommended gradual and closely supervised release into the community, with access to accommodation, employment, and suitable services (*Currie* [2009] QSC 112 at [14]; *Edwards* [2007] QSC 396 at [18]-[19]; *Fardon* [2005] QSC 137 at [113], [2006] QSC 275 at [81], [2006] QCA 512 at [18]-[19]; [2007] QSC 299 at [28]; *Hansen* [2006] QSC 35 at [23]; *HTR* [2007] QSC 19; *Levack* [2007] QSC 275 at [60]; *LSS* [2007] QSC 202 at [29]; *Robinson* [2007] QCA 111 at [9]). This issue was raised in multiple hearings involving Robert Fardon spread over a number of years, so it could not have escaped the attention of the Queensland government that Supreme Court judges regard this to be a major problem with the DPSOA. As the President of the Court of Appeal, Justice Margaret McMurdo, observed ([2006] QCA 512 at [19]):

> The fact that the community would be best protected by the respondent's graduated release from prison into the community

> on leave, presently an unavailable option in the Queensland Corrective Services system, has long concerned courts hearing applications under the Act relating to the respondent. It was raised first by White J in November 2003 [2003] QSC 379 at [55], [91], [92] and [101] and again by Moynihan J on 11 May 2005 [2005] QSC 137 at [58] and [112].

The Court of Appeal took the unusual step of requesting further details from the Attorney-General regarding the present availability of a suitable graduated release program for Robert Fardon. After an adjournment, the General Manager of Wolston Correctional Centre gave evidence that arrangements would be made to assist Fardon with counselling, post-release employment and a 'transitions' program that prepares prisoners for life in the community.

The Court of Appeal observed that 'none of these services had previously been offered to the respondent' (at [21]). After referring to a press release in which the Minister for Police and Corrective Services announced that sex offenders would no longer be accommodated in low security prison farms, and would be prohibited from engaging in community service work, the Court of Appeal observed at [23]:

> As Mr O'Gorman SC for the respondent submits, Mr Brown's evidence does not explain why the assistance to the respondent he now proposes was not offered over the past three years since the matter was first raised by White J on 6 November 2003. In any case, the program now suggested by Mr Brown involves only activities within the Wolston Correctional Centre. It is not in reality a program which would truly integrate his gradual release into the community. Furthermore, (recent legislative amendments now provide) … that a prisoner sentenced for a sexual offence is not entitled to leave of absence other than for compassionate or health leave.

Justice Kenneth Mackenzie made similar observations in *Francis* [2005] QSC 381 at [135]-[137] (to which he adhered in *Hansen* [2006] QSC 35):

> The reason for raising the issues just discussed is not to make gratuitous criticism of the Department. It is to raise an important issue, that unless procedures exist for this special class of prisoner, the difficult question of drawing the boundary between making a continuing detention order which involves further imprisonment, or a supervision order, which does not, will have to be addressed more acutely than is necessary in this case. Of all kinds of prisoners,

> this category, if ready to be integrated back into the community by staged release, will need intensive supervision at least in the early stages to ensure that the conditions of release are strictly observed. Whether increasingly sophisticated use of technology may be an answer was not explored in these proceedings, but may have to be administratively. If curfews and restrictions on lifestyle are part of the early stages of the process, it does not seem appropriate to make an order casting primary responsibility on a non-departmental agency or person to notify of potential contraventions of the terms of release.
>
> Lack of some kind of scheme under which prisoners of this category can be supervised intensively in the initial period of the stage of release is a serious deficiency. In particular, the lack of a facility in which the prisoner can reside where someone has authority to deal with and responsibility for dealing with observance of the terms of release seems to me to be a minimum requirement in the interests of the protection of the community. If that cuts across existing or proposed Departmental policy, the policy may have to be reconsidered in relation to this category of prisoner. If it requires significant commitment of resources, even though the Department may wish to deploy them in other ways, hard decisions will have to be made.
>
> If the Department provides no means of effectively staging release of this category of prisoner back into the community, it may be that decisions about whether to further deprive a person of liberty, beyond the term of imprisonment imposed when the person is originally sentenced, will have to take that into account. It will have to be put into the balance, along with the fact that preventive detention is an extraordinary sanction, the consequences that flow from it by reason that it allows potentially open-ended deprivation of liberty and the inherent element of uncertainty in predicting further offending …

In *Robinson* [2007] QCA 111, Legal Aid Queensland made a submission that DPSOA proceedings were not 'simple adversarial proceedings' and that the Supreme Court had to be more proactive when developing supervision orders to ensure that resources were made available to effect them. The Court of Appeal rejected this argument. Justice Catherine Holmes, for the court, stated at [20]-[22]:

> **The judge's responsibility to devise a supervision order**
>
> At one point in her judgment her Honour identified the relevant question in this way:

> 'The question I must answer is whether on the current information I am satisfied that the adequate protection of the community can be ensured by a Supervision Order'.

Counsel for the appellant submitted that the phrase 'on the current information' revealed error. These were not, he contended, simple adversarial proceedings. If it were possible to achieve adequate protection of the community by a supervision order, the Court was obliged to establish for itself what form of supervision order would be effective, and then to prescribe it. On the evidence before her the learned judge ought to have made further investigation as to whether a supervision order could be achieved which gave adequate protection. She ought, at least, to have required that a more detailed proposal be formulated.

Counsel put the argument in these terms:

> 'If the question is whether the protection of the community can be adequately ensured by such an order, then it should be made, and if that means it should be investigated and questions should be asked by the judge and suggestions should be made arising out of the evidence, then that's what's required by the Act'.

The submission, counsel said, was based on the examining psychiatrists' evidence: Dr Grant as to the need for strict supervision to reduce the risk of destabilisation; Professor James as to the desirability of some sort of case manager and therapist to oversee the supervision of the appellant. There should have been an enquiry into the practicability of that step.

That submission cannot, in my view, be supported by reference to anything in the *Dangerous Prisoners (Sexual Offenders) Act*. The Court is required by s 13(2) to make the finding as to whether there is an unacceptable risk that the prisoner will commit a serious sexual offence. A judge considering the making of a s 13 order must certainly consider whether a supervision order, with what conditions, can achieve community protection; and in that process it may be necessary to go beyond a draft provided by the parties. But that is a different exercise from embarking on an enquiry into resources which might be drafted to the prisoner's cause; and it was really the latter which the appellant was proposing. The learned judge would have been entitled to seek further information from the parties in that regard; but it was not incumbent on her to do more than consider, on the evidence which was before her, what level of protection could be achieved by the conditions of a supervision order.

Nevertheless, concerns have been expressed by the Supreme Court in a number of cases.

One of the most significant problems, as we stated above, has been to find suitable accommodation for supervisees. In response to the challenge presented by a growing number of released prisoners, Queensland Corrective Services has renovated a number of buildings adjacent to the Wacol Prison Reserve in outer-suburban Brisbane for use as supervisee accommodation. This accommodation is located only 20 metres from the prison and is surrounded by a 10-metre high, barbed wire fence. Twenty-four hour CCTV and floodlights have been installed (*Downs* [2008] QSC 87 at [8]). A dog squad officer has also been placed just outside the new facility as an added security measure (Moloney, 2008). All 'residents' are given a security classification rating before moving into the precinct and are required to carry Queensland Corrective Services identification cards at all times. Justice Richard Chesterman described the Wacol Prison Reserve in unflattering terms in *Toms* [2007] QSC 290 at [15]:

> [H]e was moved to accommodation at Wacol near the prison which was far less suitable. One of his neighbours was a notorious criminal and paedophile with whom the respondent was thrown in contact. The location is isolated and offers no opportunity for positive social interaction or employment. The respondent told Dr James that his location at Wacol made his anticipated rehabilitation into society more difficult and he found the consumption of alcohol alleviated his sense of isolation and rejection.

Therapeutic interventions do not appear to be the focus of activity in the Prison Reserve. In *Currie* [2009] QSC 112 at [13], the director of the High Risk Offender Management Unit within Queensland Corrective Services gave evidence that:

> Whilst some initial support is offered on a case by case basis, offenders are expected to live independently and are responsible for their own reintegration activities in accordance with the conditions of their order ... The precinct does not provide an intensive personal support program and does not include such activities as escorted leave.

The Supreme Court has exhorted Queensland Corrective Services to find better accommodation meeting the recommendations of psychiatrists 'as a matter of urgency' (*Toms* [2008] QSC 131 at [23]). However for an increasing number of prisoners there appears to be no other option for them than the Wacol Prison Reserve (*George* [2009] QSC 2 at [41]). Developing a sensible and properly funded policy for pre-release planning and post-release housing and community support for people who are released from prison is in the best interest of the community, and would therefore help to realise the DPSOA's 'paramount' concern for the protection of the community (DPSOA, s 13(6)).

In 2008, an inter-departmental working group of the Queensland government (Queensland Corrective Services, 2008) recommended that 'the practice of providing accommodation on prison property for those offenders who cannot be properly managed in a residential setting continue' (Recommendation 10) and that 'the controlled disclosure of information about prisoners released on Supervision Orders to the community be endorsed. The amount of information disclosed should be dependent upon where the offender is accommodated and the offender's risk profile' (Recommendation 12). Together, these recommendations give rise to some very serious concerns. There have been a number of well-publicised incidents in recent years where the details of residential placement arrangements for released offenders have been leaked to the media. It is not surprising that neighbours become anxious when they learn that a released offender is living nearby, and there is a real risk that this anxiety can turn into vigilantism.

The question as to whether the details of sex offenders' movements and housing arrangements should be made publicly available raises complex ethical issues and is not discussed in detail in this book (for an illuminating account, see Allen and Strossen, 1998). But it is a question that warrants thorough research, consideration and reflection. It seems obvious that the 'controlled disclosure' of information about the residential arrangements of released sex offenders could very easily become anything but 'controlled'. Once the word is out it can be spread, and this can damage attempts to reintegrate into the community (a fragile process) and may even increase the likelihood of vigilantism (Keyzer and Coyle, 2009). Although the 2008 Report by the inter-departmental working group indicated that these recommendations were accepted by the Queensland government, they did not appear in the Dangerous Prisoners (Sexual Offenders) and Other Legislation Amendment Bill 2009.

Washington State

The Provision of Treatment

Shortly after the Washington State law took effect, detainees at the special commitment centre applied for an injunction requiring the State of Washington to ensure that the centre provided constitutionally adequate treatment. Relying on the Supreme Court's general jurisprudence of due process in mental health cases, including the requirement identified by the majority in *Allen v Illinois* 478 US 364 (1986) that regard must be had to the effect of a law and not merely its text, the detainees persuaded a federal district judge in Washington State to issue an injunction requiring the State's civil commitment centre to bring its treatment program into compliance with constitutional requirements (*Turay v Richards* No C91-0664RSM, 2007 WL 983132 in Smith, 2008). The 'Turay injunction' required among other things the hiring and training of therapists, individual treatment plans and expert supervision. It required the involvement of offenders' spouses and families in therapeutic interventions as well as regular measurement of treatment outcomes and detainee progress, in order that the detainee might achieve the ultimate objective of release.

In light of continued government unwillingness to provide adequate treatment services and related supports, further litigation took place and the federal district court held that the Washington State special commitment centre had not complied with the Turay injunction (Smith, 2008). As a result, it had to spend millions of dollars upgrading its program (La Fond, 1998; Winick and La Fond, 2003). As of September 2003, it had accumulated fines in excess of $8 million that it would have to pay if it did not locate a community 12-bed halfway house for 'sexually violent predators' as ordered by a federal court. However, in 2007, the court later dissolved the injunction on the basis that it 'did not rise to the level of a constitutional violation' (Smith, 2008). The federal district court ruled that Washington State was finally in substantial compliance with the court order and set aside nearly $11 million in fines (La Fond, 2005, p 152).

Lawyers representing detainees under the Washington State system have argued persuasively that 'without adequate treatment providing a path to an individual's potential release, civil commitment becomes state-imposed criminal punishment, yet a civilly committed individual lacks the procedural protections typically afforded a criminal defendant' (Smith, 2008). Because the Supreme Court in *Seling v Young* 531 US 250 (2001) did not spell out the contours of the legal requirement of treatment in detailed terms, this has left detainees with the less powerful option of civil action against the State to enforce the statutory care and treatment requirements.

As a consequence, many people in these systems have been committed but are still awaiting trial (La Fond, 2005). In the absence of adequate treatment supports these people are very unlikely to be released, and the number of people detained will continue to grow. John La Fond has argued that pressure should be put on both prosecutors and defence counsel to bring these cases to trial within a reasonable time. On the filing of the petition, the Washington State sexually violent predator law requires that the probable-cause hearing be held within 72 hours of taking the individual into custody and that the trial be held within 45 days of the probable-cause hearing (Wash Rev Code (2002)). However, it appears that the 45-day time limit is almost *never* met (La Fond, 2005, p 157).

Lack of Unconditional Release

In Washington State not a *single* offender had been given a final unconditional release by October 2002. As John La Fond has commented, no expert ever thought that it would take over a decade to treat every single offender ever committed as a sexually violent predator (La Fond, 2005, p 149). As of July 2003, Washington State had reportedly released six men from its McNeil Island Special Commitment Centre and none of them had reoffended as of that date (La Fond, 2005, p 148). Since then, according to the Washington State Institute for Public Policy of 2005 Report on Involuntary Commitment of Sexually Violent Predators, a total of 427 people across the United States have been released onto orders called Less Restrictive Alternatives (LRAs). That means of 3493 people held under sexually violent predator laws in 2005, about 12.5 per cent had been released (Texas Department of State Health Services, 2009).

In 2008, there were 271 offenders at the special commitment centre, which has a capacity of 400. The cost of treating and confining a person in the centre was more than $169,000 per year. In 2001, Washington State commenced planning for a 'secure community transition facility'. Washington State decided to locate this next to the special commitment centre, but this proposal was rejected by the federal district court. A joint select committee of legislators was convened and, in 2002, Washington State enacted legislation that required secure community transition facilities to be created in the counties of Washington State that had committed more than five offenders to the special commitment centre. The law also pre-empted the use of local government planning regulations to thwart the creation of such facilities. As a result, several facilities have been built. At present, these facilities are undersubscribed which means the cost of operating them is very high (ranging from $400,000 to $1 million per supervisee per facility). However, it is expected that these costs will drop as the number of supervisees rises.

John La Fond has identified the many reasons why the States with sexually violent predator laws have not released offenders (La Fond, 2003, 2005). They have not built suitable facilities. They have not established systematic programs. They have balked at the expense and have not hired professional staff to build these programs. In addition, there is resistance in local communities to having a community placement facility in their midst (La Fond, 2003, 2005). On the one hand, facilities should be within or close to population centres to ensure that professional staff are located within commuting distance and detainees can access educational and employment services. On the other hand, community notification laws that restrict residential locations of released offenders may require that 'less restrictive alternative' facilities should not be close to schools, residential neighbourhoods or potential victims (La Fond, 1998, 2008). It is no surprise that without community-based residential facilities and treatment supports in place, offenders have difficulty securing release. Washington State, almost 13 years after enacting the first sexually violent predator law, finally constructed its first facility to house predators granted conditional release. As we noted above, it did so only after this was ordered by a federal judge (*Turay v Weston* No C91-664WD (WD Wash 1994)). Policy responses have been slow because politicians and policy makers need to manage community expectations and, for many in the community, the whole point of preventive detention is to confine sex offenders as long as possible (La Fond, 2005, p 146).

The Costs of Detention

States must pay a high price for preventive detention of a serious sex offender because detention regimes are extremely expensive to operate. John La Fond (2005, p 150) reports:

> In 2003, states reported per capita treatment costs ranging from \$47,555 in Florida to \$138,841 in North Dakota. These costs do not include the capital expense of building or renovating facilities to house detainees, associated expenses of a commitment system, such as compiling records of sex offenders about to be released from prison, screening those records, conducting pretrial evaluations, representing the prosecution and the defendant in probable-cause hearings and in trials and appeals, establishing a community release program, and other associated costs.

Across the country, the average annual cost to treat civilly committed sex offenders ranges from \$90,000 to \$120,000 per offender (La Fond, 2005; Schlank and Harry, 2003). Typically, the cost of treating sexual predators far exceeds the cost of incarceration. This contrasts sharply with the costs of the Texas regime for the management of sex offenders, which is an 'outpatient' model involving release, supervision and treatment in the community. On 1 June 2009 the Texas Department of State Health Services reported that their outpatient program cost Texas an average of \$26,371 per person per year.

In addition, there are the costs of litigation and the costs to the court system. One State official in Washington State estimated that court and litigation costs average about \$35,000 per patient per year. Minnesota officials have estimated that the cost of a single commitment proceeding costs about \$100,000 for attorneys and experts alone. This estimate does not include other court costs (Fitch, 2003; La Fond, 2005, p 150). States that enact sexually violent predator laws can expect at least three generations of litigation (La Fond, 1998, 2008; Harris, 2004). La Fond (2005, p 160) writes:

> The first generation will include legal challenges to the implementation of these laws, including procedural and evidentiary issues that state courts will have to resolve. The second generation will include challenges to the conditions of confinement and right to treatment lawsuits. Offenders will sue to make sure that the state provides treatment required by the Constitution and by the sexually violent predator statute. As set out above, the financial costs are immense. Finally, a third generation of lawsuits will seek the release of sexually violent predators, many of whom will stay in

facilities for most of their lives, requiring more medical services as they age.

John La Fond has stated that 'sexually violent predator laws create "black holes" that burn through cash almost as fast as failing internet companies' (La Fond, 2005, p 160). We will examine the lessons that can be learned from the United States experience in the next chapter.

Scotland

While the Scottish scheme is still relatively new, it appears that the numbers of applications for risk assessment orders as the precursor to applications for orders for lifelong restriction (OLRs) are increasing all the time. As at mid June 2009, out of 34 concluded cases, 28 offenders had been given OLRs, with a further 18 matters pending (Risk Management Authority, 2009b). Some attention has been given to the resourcing issues that have arisen in the other jurisdictions we have studied here. Multi-agency public protection arrangements (MAPPAs), implemented under the *Management of Offenders etc (Scotland) Act 2005*, came into force in Scotland in April 2007 for each of Scotland's eight community justice authority areas.

Reports for 2007-2008 show positive results for the management of sex offenders across Scotland via the interaction, implementation, structures and processes administered by the MAPPAs. These arrangements include legislative requirements that the police, prison service and local authorities and other agencies cooperate with the authorities, including health boards, Principal Reporter to the Scottish Children's Reporter Administration, housing providers which accommodate MAPPA offenders and electronic monitoring providers (Scottish Government News Site, 2008).

Despite the Scottish government's preparedness to fund risk assessors via Prison Services, there is some concern that as applications for risk assessment orders increase, there will not be enough resources to provide sufficient training and accreditation for highly qualified mental health professionals to cope with demand. Prison Services also need sufficient funding to ensure the provision of enough staff who can provide appropriate management for those on OLRs. While no individual subject to an OLR has yet been released into the community, obviously extensive community resources will be needed to supervise such individuals for the rest of their lives.

While the Risk Management Authority Board members currently oversee and regularly review every risk management plan, as the number of those on OLRs increases, this may not be viable. Consideration is currently being given to delegating the management process to certain services, with the Risk Management Authority having an auditing role. The management load on the Risk Management Authority is increasing each year and it is difficult for its members to know in advance how many more OLRs will be made by the High Court. There may be a need to streamline procedures as the numbers grow.

There are other controversial dimensions to the Scottish scheme. It alters the traditional limited role of the prosecutor in the criminal justice system. In the past, sentencing was entirely a matter for the court. Now, prosecutors must identify which individuals should be subject to an initial application for a risk assessment order. An application for such an order may contain information that goes far beyond that of the actual offence for which the person has been convicted in that it can include 'details of previous convictions, previous acquittals, allegations made to police which were not reported to the Procurator Fiscal and even intelligence information' (McFadyen, 2008, p 2). Norman McFadyen has suggested that allowing the court to consider this material enables it to gauge the 'true risk' that a person represents to the community if released (McFadyen, 2008, p 2).

However, if a person has been acquitted of a crime then the evidence is likely to have failed to satisfy the criminal standard of proof (beyond reasonable doubt). Since an acquittal involves no reflection by the judge on the question whether the evidence led would even satisfy the civil standard of proof, it is wrong to assume that it would, and therefore inappropriate to have regard to it in any decision-making context that may result in the imposition of restrictions of liberty on the accused. Where a charge has been brought and there has been no conviction, a decision maker should honour the presumption of innocence and disregard such material (*Taylor* [2008] QSC 183 at [24]; *Oliver* [2009] QSC 34 at [20]).

Allowing untried allegations to be admitted at the risk assessment order stage may also mean that certain vulnerable individuals who have made allegations that have not resulted in a prosecution, let alone a conviction, could be called to court to give evidence.

A further issue of concern is that while individuals can appeal against the making of an OLR, there is no right of appeal against the making of a risk assessment order (s 210B(6)), which raises issues of fairness for the individual concerned. It is also interesting that the prosecution has the right to appeal against the *refusal* to make an OLR (s 210F(3)).

Because the Scottish scheme thus far applies to a relatively small number of offenders, anecdotal evidence is that some lawyers have sometimes confused 'OLRs' - orders for lifelong restriction - with 'RLOs' - restriction of liberty orders which enable offenders to serve sentences in the community under certain restrictions instead of serving time in prison. Many of those under restriction of liberty orders are 'tagged' with electronic monitoring equipment to monitor their compliance with the terms of the order. The maximum time for restriction of liberty orders is 12 months and offenders under such orders are of a different ilk to high risk offenders.

Concerns have also been raised that the Scottish scheme may be inappropriately targeted at young offenders. On 11 June 2009, Thomas Lyons, 17, became the youngest person in Scotland to be given an order for lifelong restriction after he pled guilty to four charges of assault with intent to rape (The Herald, 2009). Previously, Darren Cornelius, an 18-year-old, was the youngest person to be given such an order (Howie and Pykett, 2008). Another 17-year-old, Terry Johnston, has also been referred by the Edinburgh Sheriff Court to the High Court for a possible order for lifelong restriction (STV News, 2009).

In relation to Thomas Lyons' case, while four charges of assault with intent to rape amount to serious crimes, they can nevertheless be viewed as being at the low range of the scale of such crimes. The judge ordered Lyons to serve a minimum of four and a half years. This raises the concern that some offenders may plead guilty because of the prospect of a relatively low minimum term, rather than fully understanding that they will be subject to restrictions on their liberty for the rest of their lives.

Ordering a juvenile to undergo lifelong restriction may offend the *parens patriae* principle that informs the provision of juvenile justice: that young people should be dealt with separately to adults, and every effort should be made to provide them with assistance and guidance, and minimise the potentially harmful effects of 'contamination and stigma' that come from being dealt with in the adult system

(Cunneen and White, 2007, p 14). The preparedness of judges to set relatively short minimum terms as part of OLRs also raises the spectre of 'net-widening'.

As the Scottish scheme is in its infancy, it is still unclear how and whether it will work to reduce offending. Since OLRs have only been available as a sentencing option since June 2006, all of the people who have been subject to such orders are still within the custodial element of their sentences, and will only be released when and if it is deemed that the risk that they pose to the public is at an acceptable level. However, now that judges are passing relatively short minimum terms, some offenders will be due for release in the next few years. The next phase of the process will be to see how risk management plans work in practice as and when the first offenders subject to OLRs are released from prison. There are high expectations that risk management upon release will be effective (McFadyen, 2008).

Conclusion

In this chapter, we have concentrated primarily on the problems raised throughout the implementation of the Queensland scheme. Many of the problems experienced in Queensland have been echoed in the United States. While the Scottish scheme is in its infancy, there have been some concerns raised about its use, but the development of the Risk Management Authority seems to have eased its implementation somewhat.

We suggest that because the Queensland legislation was enacted hastily, in response to the media outcry that occurred following the release of Dennis Ferguson, there was a lack of preparedness on the part of the agencies involved to cope with the intricacies of a complex and untried scheme. There has been evidence in some cases that Queensland Corrective Services is rising to meet the many challenges that have been thrown up by the legislation. But overall the picture is one of government departments who were ill-prepared, poorly resourced and therefore poorly prepared to manage. As it is expected there will be 100 people on DPSOA orders by 2010 (Queensland Corrective Services, 2008), it is imperative that the government departments charged with this important responsibility make their best efforts to, and in fact do, provide treatment and rehabilitative resources. At present it is difficult to avoid the conclusion that Queensland's principal objective has been to maintain control of offenders who have served their sentences, with positive therapeutic outcomes being an afterthought.

Indeed, this conclusion is reinforced when one considers the objects clause of the DPSOA (s 3). While the courts in *Francis* and *Lawrence* urged a reading of the DPSOA that emphasises its therapeutic objectives, it must be recognised that the objects clause of the DPSOA indicates that the formal intention of the legislation is the 'control, care *or* treatment' of offenders. As the Supreme Court observed in *Downs* [2008] QSC 87, as a matter of ordinary language, these objects must be read disjunctively. In other words, it appears to be open to a court to make an order that has nothing to do with the care or treatment of an offender, and instead is *only* based on the need to control someone considered to be a danger to the community (*Lawrence* [2008] QSC 230; *Hynds* [2007] QSC 374).

CHAPTER 5

Conclusions

In Chapter 1 we explored the case studies of three sex offenders, Earl Shriner, Dennis Ferguson and John Cronin, that gave rise to media and community pressure on three different governments to detain and monitor sex offenders. While certain groups have been targeted for removal from society throughout history, sex offenders have raised particular concerns in those societies that are grounded in the politics of risk and precaution. Preventive detention is a politically attractive tool for any government in search of legal avenues to deal with perceptions of continuing criminal behaviour (Keyzer and Blay, 2006). Preventive detention laws are an ostensible demonstration to the electorate that the government is taking serious measures to protect the community against crime.

There can be no doubt that the crimes described in Chapter 1 were horrific, and warranted severe punishment. But, as outlined in Chapter 2, the notion that all sex offenders commit crimes like this is mistaken (Lievore, 2005; Gelb, 2007). There are a number of enduring myths about sex offenders and sex offending. One is that sex offenders are more likely than other criminals to reoffend. As explored in Chapter 2, the available literature does not support this premise. Another is that most sex offenders prey on strangers. That is also incorrect. As we pointed out in Chapter 2, current research suggests that most offenders know their victims and most are never convicted for their crimes (Gelb, 2007). However, despite the growing literature debunking these myths, legislative responses have been both punitive and far-reaching. In this chapter we draw together some of our previous observations and consider a number of key issues: the impact of preventive detention regimes on human rights; the need for community-based services and treatment supports for released offenders; and ultimately, the pathway to a better system.

Preventive Detention Regimes and Human Rights

In Chapter 3, we identified a number of important criticisms concerning the impact that post-sentence preventive detention regimes have on human rights. Preventive detention schemes, such as those modelled on the Queensland and Washington schemes, that authorise the detention of a person in a punitive environment without a fresh crime or criminal trial in reality inflict double punishment. These schemes break the nexus between community censure as a component of a sentence and the crime for which a sentence is imposed. In doing so, they distort sentencing principles by altering the deterrent value of a sentence, turning finite sentences into indefinite sentences. This results in uncertainty and disturbs the calculation of proportionality that takes place in the normal sentencing process (Keyzer, Pereira and Southwood, 2004). Post-sentence preventive detention that takes place in a punitive environment is also arguably arbitrary punishment because it breaches the principle against the retrospective operation of the law, and is therefore inconsistent with the *International Covenant on Civil and Political Rights.*

The Queensland scheme in particular, by authorising the detention of sex offenders in prison after the expiry of their prison sentence, tests the boundaries of human rights protection. The *Dangerous Prisoners (Sexual Offenders) Act 2003* (Qld) would be unlikely to survive a constitutional challenge if it had been enacted in Washington State. In that jurisdiction, the United States Bill of Rights and its protections against retrospective legislation and double jeopardy could have been invoked to strike down such a law. Similarly, the Queensland law would be likely to be struck down if it were enacted in Scotland, due to the applicability of the *European Convention on Human Rights.* At present, however, Australia has no general statutory or constitutional protection of human rights, and it seems that, following *Fardon v Attorney-General (Qld)* (2004) 223 CLR 575, imprisonment can be ordered for non-punitive purposes. Communications filed with the United Nations Human Rights Committee by prisoners incarcerated under the Queensland and New South Wales preventive detention laws may ultimately lead to changes in the law. But this will of course depend on the outcome of those communications and also the willingness of the Commonwealth government to enter this regulatory field and forbid post-sentence preventive detention in prison.

While offenders detained under civil commitment laws in Washington and other States of the United States ostensibly enjoy the protection of the United States Bill of Rights, the Supreme Court of the United States rejected an attempt in *Seling v Young* 531 US 250 (2001) to enforce constitutional safeguards of due process 'as applied' in individual cases involving sex offenders. Andre Young had argued that while he had been detained in a special commitment centre, the conditions of his civil confinement were punitive in effect. However, the Supreme Court was unwilling to examine the actual conditions of his civil commitment in applying the constitutional standard of due process. This has effectively neutralised the due process standard, and left detainees with the less powerful option of securing fidelity to statutory treatment standards. It is interesting that both the Australian High Court and the United States Supreme Court have been unwilling to engage in constitutional review of the actual conditions of detention of serious sex offenders.

At face value, a system of civil commitment that authorises the imprisonment of a person, such as in Queensland, would appear to be more punitive than a system of civil commitment that authorises the detention of a person in a special facility for treatment. Ultimately, from the point of view of the detainee, much depends on the actual conditions of detention. The Supreme Court of the United States has demonstrated (increasing) reluctance to review the conditions of detention. The High Court of Australia has indicated no interest in this issue at all. But it is interesting to note that only a small minority of sexually violent predators detained under the Washington regime have been released from civil confinement. In contrast, the majority of offenders dealt with under the DPSOA are released on supervision. This last fact does not immunise the Queensland regime from criticism. The notion that prisons should be used for purposes other than housing criminals is, for the reasons we traversed in Chapter 3, contentious to say the least.

The Scottish system avoids these objections to the Queensland and Washington regimes. The order for lifelong restriction is made at the time of sentencing. Thus, there is no retrospectivity issue, and no double punishment is inflicted. There is no evidence to suggest that restrictions imposed under this regime are arbitrary. And should litigation arise in respect of the latter question, the *European Convention on Human Rights* would provide a normative reference point for review.

Of course the Queensland and Washington preventive detention regimes were introduced because of a perceived gap in the system – a device enabling the further detention of convicted sex offenders who may not satisfy a test of mental illness. As Williams JA observed in *Fardon* [2003] QCA 416 at [103]:

> Given the provisions of the [Dangerous Prisoners Sexual Offenders] Act, why could not that judge say in the course of passing sentence that indefinite detention was not justified on the material presently available, but the position should be monitored towards the end of the period in custody and if evidence was then available that the offender was a serious danger to the community the procedure provided for by the [Dangerous Prisoners Sexual Offenders] Act, should be enlivened. Senior counsel for the appellant submitted that it would be wrong for a sentencing judge to so reason, whilst the Solicitor-General responded by saying that that would be a proper course for the court to adopt. As the latter put it: 'Courts should refrain from guessing when they can know'. It seems to me that the response of the Solicitor-General is correct.

It is arguable that a post-sentence risk assessment regime has an advantage over a regime that operates at the time of sentencing because risk is tied to the offender's current state of mind and behaviour close to release. However, given that a salient predictor of future risk is past behaviour, the fact that the offender has been locked away in the artificial environment of a prison for many years poses particular difficulties for risk assessors. There are a number of advantages of the Scottish system in this regard. The Scottish system provides a basis upon which risk can be continuously monitored and assessed throughout custody and upon the expiry of a sentence. It also provides the infrastructure for treatment to be provided in the community. And once an offender has been released into the community, it affords the option of detention for breaches that might minimise risk.

Risk Assessment in Preventive Detention Matters

Traditionally, the existence of certain serious mental illnesses and the risk of harm to self or others has provided a justification for the involuntary detention and treatment of certain individuals (McSherry, 2008). The relaxation of civil commitment criteria to include those who do not have serious mental illnesses brings with it the spectre of false imprisonment. Civil commitment systems rely heavily on risk assessments conducted by psychiatrists and psychologists. As we noted in Chapter 2, these risk assessment methods are problematic. If the criteria for post-sentence commitment are relaxed to include 'mental abnormality' or 'personality disorder', then risk assessments may be yoked to vague concepts for which there are no diagnostic criteria.

Many mental health professionals do admit their capacity to predict risk is limited (Mercado and Ogloff, 2007). However, actuarial risk assessment instruments carry the promise (if not the reality) of increased accuracy; some have argued that the use of such instruments is more reliable than clinical judgments. If mental health professionals using these tools are highly qualified and prepare reports containing persuasive material, then it easy to see why judges would order the continuing detention of sex offenders.

In our opinion, expert witnesses have an ethical obligation to point to the limitations of the 'science' of risk prediction in every case. We note that there is little evidence in the preventive detention cases in Australia of the sort of scepticism reflected in the research literature on this topic. The preventive detention of sex offenders carries with it the risk of false positives, net widening and, in light of the statistics on recidivism, unnecessary social control. The Queensland regime, in particular, contemplates that an offender can be returned to prison purely for the purpose of control (Keyzer, 2009b). This consequence, along with the abandonment of the criminal standard of proof for detention in all three preventive detention and supervision schemes, underscores both the significance of evidence from mental health professionals and the need to ensure adequate safeguards.

The advantage of the Scottish scheme is that the Risk Management Authority not only accredits risk assessors, it also sets high standards and guidelines for risk assessment reports. In addition, while the Scottish system depends on proof to a civil standard of 'the balance of probabilities', it at least operates from the start of offenders' sentences so that they know that treatment will be offered and that their liberty will be curtailed in some form for the rest of their lives.

Reforming Sentencing

In light of the continuing debate in the United States as to the adequacy of sexually violent predator laws meeting constitutional requirements of due process, and the problems associated with operating and resourcing civil commitment programs, it has been argued that increasing criminal penalties for crimes of sexual violence may be a better option (Smith, 2008). As Levesque (2000, p 339) pointed out in his review of sentencing practices of sex offenders in the United States:

> Although the current research suggests a need for post-conviction control mechanisms, it also does seem fair to conclude that there would be a reduced need for such measures if the system did actually sentence the most serious and repeat offenders to more severe sentences, a point highlighted by the numerous times the legal system had convicted but quickly released the offender who eventually permitted the Supreme Court to find civil post-conviction sanctions permissible.

It may be that the recent wave of preventive detention laws that have emerged in Australia are, in part, a response to popular opinion that sentencing is too lenient. Substantial recent research in Australia suggests that the community perceives prison sentences to be too light (Jones, Weatherburn and Macfarlane, 2008). Recently, Marion Goddard observed that 'child abuse sentencing in Australia is soft in comparison with the rest of the world ... the sentencing does not reflect the seriousness of the crime or the damage done' (Goddard, 2009). This is an understandable response to the terrible crimes of serious sex offenders.

Sentencing reforms may be necessary to ensure that preventive detention regimes are not being used merely to extend punishment which the majority of the public feels is inadequate. John La Fond (2005) has recommended that jurisdictions with inadequate criminal sentences for serious sex offenders should enact special laws that authorise an indefinite sentence on a second offence. It is interesting to note that Queensland already has legislation authorising indefinite sentences (*Penalties and Sentences Act 1992* (Qld) ss 162-163 and *Criminal Code* (Qld) ss 208, 215, 216, 349 and 352). In addition, section 18 of the *Criminal Law Amendment Act 1945* (Qld) provides for the indeterminate detention of offenders convicted of sexual offences, on the basis of medical evidence that the offender cannot control his or her sexual instincts. John La Fond (2005, p 215) has observed that Washington has adopted an approach that approximates indefinite sentencing for recidivists, called 'determinate plus sentencing'.

Liz Richardson and Arie Freiberg have observed that Australian courts are reluctant to order indefinite sentences (Richardson and Freiberg, 2004). However, it may be that popular views on the need for longer sentences have now eclipsed judicial perceptions of proportionality in sentencing sex offenders. The New South Wales Parliament has recently accepted recommendations of its Sentencing Council to expand the range of sexual offences and increase penalties for those offences (New South Wales Sentencing Council, 2008). Perhaps one way of ameliorating the need for post-sentence preventive detention is to ensure criminal sentences are adequate.

Increasing sentences does not challenge civil liberties principles in the same way that post-sentence preventive detention does. There are also no obvious constitutional issues: constitutionally, sentencing has always occupied a unique position that straddles the exercise of legislative and judicial power. Mandatory sentencing and indefinite sentencing are constitutional. However, as with any other criminal sentencing matter, the principle of proportionality - that the punishment must fit the crime - is warranted. While all sex offences are deplorable, not every sex offence is of equal seriousness. This needs to be reflected in sentencing principles. Indefinite sentencing should be reserved for persistent offenders.

Improving and Resourcing Reintegration Policies

Public concern about the circumstances of the release of sex offenders is completely justified. Governments should be doing everything they can to decrease the risk that sex offenders will reoffend upon release. But at present, efforts to do this have been problematic.

As outlined in Chapter 4, Queensland was poorly prepared for the DPSOA and its departments were and appear to remain inadequately resourced to manage the challenge of treating and supervising sex offenders. They have struggled to cope. The DPSOA has produced significant new burdens for government departments and the courts. In a number of cases this has meant that prisoners have been detained simply because there are no suitable services and facilities in the community.

The objectives of reintegration and release into the community, respect for the principles underpinning the criminal justice system and post-sentence 'detention' as a last resort would be more likely to be realised if governments funded a system of community-based treatment programs involving qualified, independent experts to treat and supervise people who have been released from prison. This would be likely to decrease the risk that an offender might reoffend. If judges felt confident that accommodation, employment, social services and treatment supports were available in the community, this would affect their assessment of the risk that sex offenders represent upon their release. It is unfair to place prisoners who are about to be released in a situation where the only services they can access that would decrease their risk (a sex offender treatment program involving group therapy) are available in prison. And yet this is exactly how the DPSOA operates.

Energy and resources should be expended to improve and expand sex offender treatment programs so that they are available to more prisoners throughout their sentences. This would decrease the number of people who the courts believe should be reimprisoned or redetained after the conclusion of their sentences. In addition, as is the case in Scotland, treatment should be made available soon after conviction, because treatment offered at this stage is regarded to be much more effective than treatment delayed until the end of an offender's prison term (Wettstein, 1992).

Ironically enough, as explored in Chapter 4, there is more evidence that secure housing and support services outside the prison reduce recidivism than there is evidence that prison-based sex offender treatment programs reduce recidivism. We do not argue that sex offender treatment programs in the prison should be abandoned. To the contrary, they should be made available to every affected prisoner, preferably in the prison in which he or she resides. Treatment programs should be thoroughly and independently researched and analysed with the objective of improving them. However, it is important that Corrective Services do not merely focus on services available within the prison, but ensure that services are available in the community, which is where, after all, released offenders may pose a greater risk.

In Queensland, the Wacol Prison Reserve is a band-aid, not a cure for the problem of accommodating released offenders. It is too far from necessary services to enable released offenders to reintegrate effectively into the community. Treatment supports and services need to be made available there, to assist reintegration. The objective of the DPSOA is to protect the community. It is more likely that this will be achieved if proper transitional housing and social services are resourced and developed.

There are approximately 840 sex offenders in custody and about 600 sex offenders on community supervision orders in Queensland (Queensland Corrective Services, 2009). Between 2006-2007 and 2007-2008, the number of defendants proven guilty of sex offences decreased from 559 to 537, however the number sentenced to custody in a correctional institution increased from 339 to 402 (Australian Bureau of Statistics, 2009). More and more people will be released into the community under the DPSOA. The Queensland government needs to develop long-term solutions to the challenge of locating post-release housing for released offenders. The recent media attention given to Dennis Ferguson's housing arrangements highlights the need for well thought out responses. What happens in Scotland once those on orders for lifelong restriction are released into the community will provide an interesting example in this regard.

Resourcing Issues

Australian statistics indicate that sexual offences make up a small percentage of crimes generally. Across Australia in 2004-2005, of the 14,428 defendants with an adjudicated outcome in the higher courts, 13 per cent had a principal offence of sexual assault. Of these, 24 per cent were acquitted, 58 per cent pleaded guilty and 18 per cent were found guilty. For the 1383 who were proven guilty, 88 per cent were given a custodial order and 12 per cent were given a non-custodial order (Australian Bureau of Statistics, 2006). Sex offenders are more likely to receive custodial orders than non-sex offenders. In Australia in 2005, there were 18,172 victims of sexual assault recorded by the police. This represented some 1.7 per cent of all victims recorded by the police in that year.

However, as we noted in Chapter 4, almost 8 per cent of the matters determined by the Supreme Court of Queensland in 2008 were cases involving the *Dangerous Prisoners (Sexual Offenders) Act 2003*. This number is likely to grow over time, as will the number in New South Wales and Western Australia. Indeed, there are many more sex offenders in New South Wales than there are in Queensland (New South Wales has a larger population), and New South Wales is at an earlier stage in its history with this legislation.

It is also concerning that in Scotland the number of applications for lifelong restriction orders has risen exponentially in the past year. This may partly be as a result of a growing familiarity with the scheme, but there are concerns that there is some net widening occurring in relation to those considered to be high risk offenders. As pointed out in the previous chapter, the fact that 17-year-olds are being given orders for lifelong restriction raises questions of compliance with the *European Convention on Human Rights.*

It should be stressed that we are not suggesting that the consequences of these crimes are insignificant or that the amount of attention being given to this issue is unwarranted. As Marc Galanter (1983, p 35) has pointed out, an increase in the volume of legal disputes may 'contain the seeds of vindication, justice, even social improvement'. However, these statistics serve to underscore a different point. By definition, the Queensland model of preventive detention focuses attention and resources on *convicted* offenders. This may mean that we are placing resources into managing a small group of sex offenders when resources could be better expended on measures that could target the majority of sex offenders, most of whom are not charged and who go untreated (Chung, O'Leary and Hand, 2006; Miethe, Olson and Mitchell, 2006). In light of the growing body of evidence that many sex offences go undetected, uninvestigated and unprosecuted, a strong case can be made for the investment of public resources into sex offence awareness and education campaigns to curb the amount of sex offending in the community.

Conclusion

John La Fond (2005, p 165) has summarised his criticism of the United States sexually violent predator laws in the following way:

> SVP laws are fatally flawed – morally, economically, and practically. They corrupt concepts of responsibility and illness, allow preventive detention under the guise of treatment, and drain scarce resources away from law-abiding citizens who are truly mentally ill and desperately need mental health services. These laws, at best, are only a bandage solution to a fundamental structural problem in the criminal justice system. Because they are so extraordinarily expensive, and will become more expensive, they can hope to control only a relatively small number of sex offenders. SVP laws should be repealed as soon as possible. Instead, states should spend

> more money on keeping very dangerous sex offenders locked up longer and on providing effective risk-management programs to monitor many more sex offenders living in the community.

Ultimately, the criminal justice system can protect society against very dangerous sex offenders more effectively and at much less cost via strengthening sentencing laws or by following the Scottish model of orders for lifelong restriction. Bill Hebenton and Toby Seddon (2009, p 358) point out that there is a paradox in that 'the limitless pursuit of security can end up subverting security and justice in deeply damaging ways'. The preventive detention of suspected terrorists has taken centre stage in public debates about the punitive power of the state. But there are more sex offenders and victims of sex offenders than there are terrorists and victims of terrorists. There is a need to educate the community about the issues in this vitally important area of public policy.

The problem with preventive detention laws is that they may start out as 'exceptional' measures to combat community fears of what David Garland (1996, p 461) has termed the 'alien other'. However, exceptional measures have a tendency to become the norm over an extended period of time (Agamben, 2005). It is important therefore to continue questioning whether preventive detention and supervision laws provide the most adequate response to the realities of sexual abuse in society. In our view, the disadvantages outweigh the advantages of post-sentence preventive detention. The Scottish scheme avoids many of the human rights issues raised by the Queensland and Washington models, but it is by no means without flaws.

As indicated in Chapter 2, the selective detention of those considered dangerous is not a new phenomenon and will no doubt continue in different guises. While preventive detention laws may protect the public from a handful of sex offenders, they are a politically attractive method of responding to media and community concerns that ultimately detracts from other more viable and evidence-based means of managing sex offenders and reducing sexual offences in the community.

References

ABC News Online, (2009) 'Paedophile Dennis Ferguson Evicted' 24 September 2009 <http://www.abc.net.au/news/stories/2009/09/24/2695726.htm>.

ABC 'PM' radio program, (2003) 'Queensland Looks at Laws as Paedophile Released' 9 January 2003.

ABC Stateline Queensland, (2008) 'Ferguson Fuss' 11 July 2008.

Agamben, G, (2005) *State of Exception* Chicago: University of Chicago Press.

Alexander, Matilda, (2009) Prisoners Legal Service (Queensland), Personal Communication to Professor Keyzer, 3 March 2009.

Allen, E and Strossen, N, (1998) 'Megan's Law and the Protection of the Child in the On-Line Age' 35 *American Criminal Law Review* 1319-1341.

American Psychiatric Association, (2009) 'The Principles of Medical Ethics With Annotations Especially Applicable to Psychiatry' American Psychiatric Association, United States.

Appelbaum, PS, (1984) 'Psychiatric Ethics in the Courtroom' 12 *Bulletin of the American Academy of Psychiatry and Law* 225-231.

Appelbaum, PS, (1990) 'The Parable of the Forensic Psychiatrist: Ethics and the Problem of Doing Harm' 13 *International Journal of Law and Psychiatry* 249-259.

Appelbaum, PS, (1997a) 'A Theory of Ethics for Forensic Psychiatry' 25 *The Journal of the American Academy of Psychiatry and the Law* 233-246.

Appelbaum, PS, (1997b) 'Confining Sex Offenders: The Supreme Court Takes a Dangerous Path' 48(10) *Psychiatric Services* 1265-1267.

Appelbaum, PS, (2005) 'Dangerous Severe Personality Disorders: England's Experiment in Using Psychiatry for Public Protection' 56(4) *Psychiatric Services* 397-399.

Appelbaum, PS, (2008) 'Ethics and Forensic Psychiatry: Translating Principles into Practice' 36(2) *The Journal of the American Academy of Psychiatry and the Law* 195-200.

Ashworth, A, (2009) 'Criminal Law, Human Rights and Preventative Justice' in B McSherry, A Norrie and S Bronitt (eds) *Regulating Deviance: The Redirection of Criminalisation and the Futures of Criminal Law,* Hart Publishing, Portland, 87-108.

Associated Press, (2005) 'Mutilation Victim Dies in Accident' *The Seattle Times,* 23 June 2005.

Australian Bureau of Statistics, (2009) *Criminal Courts in Queensland, 2007-2008 (Feature Article),* Catalogue 1318.3 - Qld Stats, Apr 2009 (22 May 2009) <http://www.abs.gov.au/AUSSTATS/abs@.nsf/Lookup/1318.3Feature%20 Article14Apr%202009>.

Australian Bureau of Statistics, (2006a) *Criminal Courts Australia, 2004-05*, Catalogue 4513.0 - Criminal Courts, Australia, 2007-08 <http://www.abs.gov.au/ausstats/abs@.nsf/Latestproducts/4513.0Main%20Features12007-08?opendocument&tabname=Summary&prodno=4513.0&issue=2007-08&num=&view=>.

Baldry, Eileen, Desmond McDonnell, Peter Maplestone and Manu Peters, (2002) 'Ex-Prisoners and Accommodation: What Bearing do Different Forms of Housing have on Social Reintegration of Ex-Prisoners?' (paper presented at the Housing, Crime and Stronger Communities Conference, Australian Institute of Criminology and the Australian Housing and Urban Research Institute, Melbourne, 6-7 May 2002).

Bar-On, D, (2001) 'The Silence of Psychologists' 22(2) *Political Psychology* 331-345.

Barry J, (1969) *The Courts and Criminal Punishments*, Government Printer, Wellington.

BBC News, (2008) 'Serial Offender Cronin Faces Jail' 20 August 2008 <http://news.bbc.co.uk/1/hi/scotland/edinburgh_and_east/6955571.stm>.

Berlin, FS, Galbreath, NW, Geary, B and McGlone, G, (2003) 'The Use of Actuarials at Civil Commitment Hearings to Predict the Likelihood of Future Sexual Violence' 15(4) *Sexual Abuse: A Journal of Research and Treatment* 377-382.

Berliner, L, Miller, LL, Schram, D and Milloy, CD, (1991) *The Special Sex Offender Sentencing Alternative: A Study of Decision-Making and Recidivism*, Report to the Legislature <http://www.wsipp.wa.gov/rptfiles/soff_alternative.pdf>.

Birmingham, L, (2002) 'Detaining Dangerous People with Mental Disorders: New Legal Framework is Open for Consultation' 325 *British Medical Journal* 2-3.

Blacher, R, (1995) 'Historical Perspective of the "Sex Psychopath" Statute: From the Revolutionary Era to the Present Federal Crime Bill' 46 *Mercer Law Review* 889-912.

Blay S and Piotrowicz R, (2001) 'The Awfulness of Lawfulness: Some Reflections on the Tension between International Law and Domestic Law' 21 *Australian Yearbook of International Law* 1-20.

Bochnewich, MA, (1992-1993) 'Prediction of Dangerousness and Washington's Sexually Violent Predator Statute' 29 *California Western Law Review* 277-306.

Bodine, BG, (1990) 'Washington's New Violent Sexual Predator Commitment System: An Unconstitutional Law and An Unwise Policy' 14 *University of Puget Sound Law Review* 105-141.

Boer, DP, Hart, SD, Kropp, PR and Webster, CD, (1997) *Manual for the Sexual Violence Risk-20*, The British Columbia Institute Against Family Violence, Vancouver, BC.

Boerner, D, (1991-1992) 'Confronting Violence: In the Act and in the Word' 15 *University of Puget Sound Law Review* 525-577.

Borzycki, M and Baldry, E, (2003) 'Promoting Integration: The Provision of Prisoner Post-release Services', Australian Institute of Criminology, Trends and Issues in Crime and Criminal Justice, No 262.

Britten, N, (2001) 'Sex Offenders May be Tracked for Life by Satellite Spy' *Telegraph* 19 June 2001 <http://www.telegraph.co.uk/news/uknews/1345154/Sex-offenders-may-be-tracked-for-life-by-satellite-spy.html>.

Bronitt S and McSherry B, (2005) *Principles of Criminal Law* Pyrmont, NSW: Lawbook Company.

Bronitt, S, (2003) 'Australia's Legal Response to Terrorism: Neither Novel nor Extraordinary?' (paper presented at the Castan Centre for Human Rights Law, Human Rights 2003: The Year in Review Conference, Melbourne, 4 December 2003).

Campbell T, (2003) 'Sex Offenders and Actuarial Risk Assessments: Ethical Considerations' 21(2) *Behavioral Sciences and the Law* 269-279.

Campbell, TW, (2000) 'Sexual Predator Evaluations and Phrenology: Considering Issues of Evidentiary Reliability' 18 *Behavioral Sciences and the Law* 111-130.

Campbell, TW, (2003) 'Sex Offenders and Actuarial Risk Assessments: Ethical Considerations' 21 *Behavioral Sciences and the Law* 269-279.

Carlsmith KM, Monahan J, and Evans A, (2007) 'The Function of Punishment in the "Civil" Commitment of Sexually Violent Predators' (2007) 25 *Behavioural Sciences and the Law* 437-448.

Carroll, A, Lyall, M and Forrester, A, (2004) 'Clinical Hopes and Public Fears in Forensic Mental Health' 15(3) *The Journal of Forensic Psychiatry and Psychology* 407-425.

Carter, D, (1990) 'Shriner Must Never Go Free, Judge Rules' *Seattle Post-Intelligencer* 27 March 1990.

Catholic Prison Ministry and Prisoners Legal Service, (2008) *Report on Queensland Prisons* <http://www.ces.org.au>.

Cavadino, M, (1998) 'Death to the Psychopath' 9(1) *Journal of Forensic Psychiatry* 5-8.

Child Protection (Offender Prohibition Order) Act 2008 (Qld).

Child Protection (Offenders Registration) Act 2000 (NSW).

Chung, D, O'Leary P and Hand, T, (2006) *Sexual Violence Offenders: Prevention and Intervention Approaches,* Australian Centre for the Study of Sexual Assault, Melbourne.

Coid, J and Maden, T, (2003) 'Should Psychiatrists Protect the Public? A New Risk Reduction Strategy, Supporting Criminal Justice, Could be Effective' 326 *British Medical Journal* 406-407.

Committee on Serious Violent and Sexual Offenders, (2000) Report SE/2000/68 <http://www.scotland.gov.uk/maclean/docs/svso.pdf>.

Community Protection Act 1990 (Wash Laws 101-1406).

Cooke, DJ and Michie, M, (2009) 'Limitations of Diagnostic Precision and Predictive Utility in the Individual Case: A Challenge for Forensic Practice' (2009) *Law and Human Behavior*. (Published Online 11 March 2009) <doi:10.1007/s10979-009-9176-x>.

Corbett, K and Westwood, T, (2005) 'Dangerous and Severe Personality Disorder: A Psychiatric Manifestation of the Risk Society' 15(2) *Critical Public Health* 121-133.

Corrective Services Act 2006 (Qld).

Coyle, IR, (2008) 'Pre-sentence Reports and Risk Assessment' in K Frizton and P Wilson (eds) *Forensic Psychology and Criminology: An Australian Perspective*, Sydney: McGraw-Hill Australia, 252-266.

Crimes (Serious Sex Offenders) Act 2006 (NSW).

Criminal Code (Qld).

Criminal Justice (Scotland) Act 2003.

Criminal Law Amendment Act 1945 (Qld).

Criminal Offences Victims Act 1995 (Qld).

Criminal Procedure (Scotland) Act 1995.

Cunneen, C and White, R, (2007), *Juvenile Justice – Youth and Crime in Australia*, Melbourne: Oxford University Press.

Dangerous Prisoners (Sexual Offenders) Act 2003.

Dangerous Prisoners (Sexual Offenders) and Other Legislation Amendment Bill 2009.

Dangerous Sexual Offenders Act 2006 (WA).

Darjee, R and Crichton, J, (2002) 'The MacLean Committee: Scotland's Answer to the Dangerous People with Severe Personality Disorder Proposals?' 26 *Psychiatric Bulletin* 6-8.

Demleitner, NV, (2003) 'Abusing State Power or Controlling Risk?: State Offender Commitment and *Sicherungverwahrung*' 30 *Fordham Urban Law Journal* 1621-1669.

Desmond, R, (2008) 'Pedophile "May End Up On Streets"' *Queensland News.Com.Au* 7 July 2008 <http://www.news.com.au/story/0,23982846-1248,00.html>.

Di Furia, G and Mees, HL, (1963) 'Dangerous to Be At Large – A Constructive Critique of Washington's Sexual Psychopath Law' 38 *Washington Law Review* 531-537.

Dick, PK, (1956) 'The Minority Report' 4(6) *Fantastic Universe* 4-36.

Douglas H, (2008) 'Post-sentence Preventive Detention: Dangerous and Risky', *Criminal Law Review* 854-873.

DSPD Programme, (2009) 'Dangerous People with Severe Personality Disorder (DSPD) A joint initiative between the Department of Health, NOMS and the Ministry of Justice' <http://www.dspdprogramme.gov.uk/index.html accessed 23 March 2009>.

Edgley M, (2007) 'Preventing Crime or Punishing Propensities? A Purposive Examination of Sex Offenders in Queensland and Western Australia' 33(2) *University of Western Australia Law Review* 351-386.

Eigen, JP, (1995) Witnessing Insanity: Madness and Mad-Doctors in the English Court, New Haven: Yale University Press.

Ellard, J, (1996) 'Personality Disorder or the Snark Still at Large' 4(2) *Australasian Psychiatry* 58-64.

Ericson, R, (2005) 'Governing Through Risk and Uncertainty' 34(4) *Economy and Society* 659-672.

Ericson, R, (2007) *Crime in an Insecure World*, Cambridge: Polity Press.

Ericson, R and Haggerty, K, (1997) *Policing the Risk Society*, Oxford: Oxford University Press.

European Convention on Human Rights, Opened for Signature 4 November 1950, CETS No 005 (entered into force 3 September 1953).

Ewald, F, (2002) 'The Return of Descartes' Malicious Demon: An Outline of a Philosophy of Precaution' in T Baker and J Simon (eds) *Embracing Risk: The Changing Culture of Insurance and Responsibility*, Chicago: The University of Chicago Press, 273-301.

Ewing, C, (1991) 'Preventive Detention and Execution: The Constitutionality of Punishing Future Crimes' 15 *Law and Human Behavior* 139-163.

Expert Panel on Sex Offending, (2001) *Reducing the Risk: Improving the Response to Sex Offending*, Report of the Expert Panel on Sex Offending, Scotland, Chaired by Lady Cosgrove <http://194.247.95.101/Publications/2001/06/9284/File-1>.

Explanatory Memorandum, (2003) *Dangerous Prisoners (Sexual Offenders) Bill 2003* (Qld).

Farnham, F and James, D, (2001) '"Dangerousness" and Dangerous Law' 358 *The Lancet* 1926.

Feeley, M and Simon, J, (1992) 'The New Penology: Notes on the Emerging Strategy of Corrections and its Implications' 30(4) *Criminology* 449-474.

Feeley, M and Simon, J, (1994) 'Actuarial Justice: The Emerging New Criminal Law' in D Nelken (ed) *The Futures of Criminology*, London: Sage Publications Ltd, 173-201.

Fitch, W Lawrence, (2003) 'Sexual Offender Commitment in the United States - Legislative and Policy Concerns' 989 *Annals New York Academy of Sciences* 489-501.

Fitch, WL and Ortega, RJ, (2000) 'Law and the Confinement of Psychopaths' 18(5) *Behavioral Sciences and the Law* 663-678.

Foster, G, (1989) 'Mutilation Suspect Denies All Charges; Spectators Cheer as Judge Sets High Bail' *Seattle Post-Intelligencer*, 23 May 1989.

Galanter, M, (1983) 'Reading the Landscape of Disputes: What We Know and Don't Know (and Think We Know) About Our Allegedly Contentious and Litigious Society' 31 *University of California Los Angeles Law Review* 4-71.

Gani, M and Mathew, P (eds), (2008) *Fresh Perspectives on the 'War on Terror'*, Canberra: ANU E Press.

Gardiner, SM, (2006) 'A Core Precautionary Principle' 14(1) *The Journal of Political Philosophy* 33-60.

Garland, D, (1996) 'The Limits of the Sovereign State' 36(4) *British Journal of Criminology* 445-471.

Gelb, K, (2007) *Recidivism of Sex Offenders: Research Paper*, Sentencing Advisory Council, Melbourne.

Gleb, G, (1991) 'Washington's Sexually Violent Predator Law: The Need to Bar Unreliable Psychiatric Predictions of Dangerousness from Civil Commitment Proceedings' 39 *UCLA Law Review* 213-250.

Glover, D, (1989) 'Forum is Outlet for Outrage' *Seattle Post-Intelligencer* 31 May 1989.

Goddard, Chris, (2009) 'Pedophile Jail Terms "Too Light" ' <http://www.theaustralian.news.com.au/story/0,25197,25566530-5013404,00.html>.

Goldsmith, A, (2008) 'The Governance of Terror: Precautionary Logic and Counterterrorist Law Reform After September 11' 30(2) *Law and Policy* 141-167.

Grisso, T and Appelbaum, PS, (1992) 'Is it Unethical to Offer Predictions of Future Violence?' 16(6) *Law and Human Behavior* 621-633.

Grounds, A, (2005) 'Forensic Psychiatry and Political Controversy' 32 *Journal of the American Academy of Psychiatry and Law* 192-196.

Gutheil, TG, (2005) 'The History of Forensic Psychiatry' 33 *Journal of the American Academy of Psychiatry and Law* 259-262.

Haddock, A, Snowden, PR, Dolan, M, Parker, J and Rees, H, (2001) 'Managing Dangerous People with Severe Personality Disorder: A Survey of Forensic Psychiatrists' Opinions' 25 *Psychiatric Bulletin* 293-296.

Hanks P, Keyzer P, and Clarke J, (2004) *Australian Constitutional Law; Materials and Commentary* Sydney: Lexis Nexis.

Hanson, RK, (2003) 'Who is Dangerous and When are They Safe? Risk Assessment with Sex Offenders' in B Winick and J La Fond (eds) *Protecting Society from Sexually Dangerous Offenders – Law, Justice and Therapy,* Washington: American Psychological Association.

Hanson, RK and Bussière, MT, (1998) 'Predicting Relapse: A Meta-analysis of Sexual Offender Recidivism Studies' 66 *Journal of Consulting and Clinical Psychology* 348-362.

Hanson, RK and Harris, AJR, (2000) 'The Sex Offender Need Assessment Rating (SONAR): A Method for Measuring Change in Risk Levels' (User Report 2000-01), Department of the Solicitor General of Canada, Ottawa.

Hanson, RK and Morton-Bourgon, K, (2004) *Predictors of Sexual Recidivism: An Updated Meta-Analysis* (User Report 2004-02), Public Safety and Emergency Preparedness Canada, Ottawa.

Hanson, RK and Thornton, D, (1999) 'Static-99: Improving Actuarial Risk Assessments for Sex Offenders' (User Report 2000-01), Department of the Solicitor General of Canada, Ottawa <http://www.static99.org/> .

Hanson, RK, Harris, AJR, Scott, T and Helmus, L, (2007) *Assessing the Risk of Sexual Offenders on Community Supervision: The Dynamic Supervision Project* (Report 2007-05) Public Safety Canada.

Hare, RD, (1991) *The Hare Psychopathy Checklist – Revised* (1st ed), Toronto: Multi-Health Systems.

Hare, RD, (2002) 'Psychopathy and Risk for Recidivism and Violence' in N Gray, J Laing and L Noaks (eds) *Criminal Justice, Mental Health and the Politics of Risk,* London: Cavendish Publishing Ltd, 27-47.

Harris, A and Hanson, RK, (2004) *Sex Offender Recidivism: A Simple Question* (No 2004-03). Ottawa: Public Safety and Emergency Preparedness Canada.

Hart, SD, Kropp, PR, Laws, DR, Klaver, J, Logan, C and Watt, KA, (2003) *The Risk of Sexual Violence Protocol (RSVP): Structured Professional Guidelines for Assessing Risk of Sexual Violence*, Vancouver BC: The British Columbia Institute Against Family Violence.

Hart, D, Michie, C and Cooke, DJ, (2007) 'Precision of Actuarial Risk Instruments: Evaluating the Margins for Error of Group Versus Individual Predictions of Violence' 190(49) *British Journal of Psychiatry* 60-65.

Hassan, P, (1973) 'The International Covenant on Civil and Political Rights: Background and Perspective on Article 9(1)' 3 *Denver Journal of International Law and Policy* 153-183.

Hawkins, G, (1986) *Prisoners' Rights: A Study of Human Rights and Commonwealth Prisoners*, Occasional Paper No 12 of the Australian Human Rights Commission, Canberra: AGPS.

Hayes, R, Barnett, M, Sullivan, DH, Nielssen, O, Large, M and Brown, C, (2009) 'Justifications and Rationalizations for the Civil Commitment of Sex Offenders' 16(1) *Psychiatry, Psychology and Law* 1-9.

Hebenton, B and Seddon, T, (2009) 'From Dangerousness to Precaution: Managing Sexual and Violent Offenders in an Insecure and Uncertain Age' 49 *British Journal of Criminology* 343-362.

Heilbrun, K, Ogloff, JRP and Picarello, K, (1999) 'Dangerous Offender Statutes in the United States and Canada: Implications for Risk Assessment' 22(3-4) *International Journal of Law and Psychiatry* 393-415.

Hogg, R, (2007) 'Criminology, Crime and Politics Before and After 9/11' 40(1) *The Australian and New Zealand Journal of Criminology* 83-105.

Howie, M and Pykett, E, (2008) 'The Teenage Crimewave the State Could Not Stop' *The Scotsman* 20 May 2008 <http://news.scotsman.com/youthcrime/The-teenage-crimewave-the-state.4099212.jp>.

Hudson, B, (2003) *Justice in the Risk Society*, London: Sage Publications Ltd.

International Covenant on Civil and Political Rights, Opened for signature 16 December 1966, 999 UNTS 171 (entered into force 23 March 1976).

Janus E, (2004) 'Closing Pandora's Box: Sexual Predators and the Politics of Sexual Violence' 34 *Seton Hall Law Review* 1233-1253.

Janus, ES, (2004a) 'The Preventive State, Terrorists and Sexual Predators: Countering the Threat of a New Outsider Jurisprudence' 40(6) *Criminal Law Bulletin* 576-598.

Janus, ES, (2004b) 'Sexually Violent Predator Laws: Psychiatry in Service to a Morally Dubious Enterprise' 364 *The Lancet* 50-51.

Janus, ES, (2006) *Failure to Protect: America's Sexual Predator Laws and the Rise of the Preventive State*, Ithaca: Cornell University Press.

Janus, ES and Prentky RA, (2003) 'Forensic Use of Actuarial Risk Assessment with Sex Offenders: Accuracy, Admissibility and Accountability' 40 *American Criminal Law Review* 1443-1500.

Johnson, B, (2005) 'Prophecy with Numbers' 7 *University of Technology, Sydney Law Review* 117-133.

Kenworthy, T, Adams, CE, Bilby, C, Brooks-Gordon B and Fenton, M, (2007) 'Psychological Interventions for Those Who Have Sexually Offended or are at Risk of Offending' *Cochrane Database of Systematic Reviews*, Issue 3, DOI: 10.1002/14651858.CD004858.

Keyzer P, (2005) *Constitutional Law*, Sydney: Lexis Nexis.

Keyzer P, (2008) 'Preserving Due Process or Warehousing the Undesirables: To What End the Separation of Judicial Power of the Commonwealth?' 30(1) *The Sydney Law Review* 104-105.

Keyzer P, (2009a) 'The "Preventive Detention" of Serious Sex Offenders: Further Consideration of the International Human Rights Dimensions' 16(2) *Psychiatry, Psychology and Law* 262-270.

Keyzer P, (2009b) 'The Dangerous Prisoners (Sexual Offenders) Act - Are "The Best Available Rehabilitative Resources" Available?' 33 *Criminal Law Journal* 175-179.

Keyzer P and Blay S, (2006) 'Double Punishment? Preventive Detention Schemes Under Australian Legislation and their Consistency with International Law: The *Fardon* Communication', 7 *Melbourne Journal of International* Law 407-422.

Keyzer, P and Coyle, I, (2009) 'Reintegrating Sex Offenders into the Community - Queensland's Proposed Reforms' 34(1) *Alternative Law Journal* 27-31.

Keyzer, P, Pereira, C and Southwood, S, (2004) 'Pre-emptive Imprisonment for Dangerousness in Queensland under the *Dangerous Prisoners (Sexual Offenders) Act* 2003: The Constitutional Issues' 11 *Psychiatry, Psychology and Law* 244-253.

Keyzer, P and O'Toole, S, (2006) 'Time, Delay and Nonfeasance - The *Dangerous Prisoners (Sexual Offenders) Act 2003* (Queensland)' 31(4) *Alternative Law Journal* 198-202.

La Fond, JQ, (2005) *Preventing Sexual Violence: How Society Should Cope with Sex Offenders*, USA: American Psychological Association.

La Fond, JQ, (1998) 'The Costs of Enacting a Sexual Predator Law' 4(1/2) *Psychology, Public Policy, and Law* 468-504.

La Fond, JQ, (2003) 'The Costs of Enacting a Sexual Predator Law and Recommendations for Keeping Them from Skyrocketing' in B Winick and JQ La Fond (eds) *Protecting Society from Sexually Dangerous Offenders: Law, Justice and Therapy*, Washington DC: American Psychological Association.

La Fond, JQ, (2008) 'Sexually Violent Predator Laws and the Liberal State: An Ominous Threat to Individual Liberty' 31(2) *International Journal of Law and Psychiatry* 158-171.

Lees, M, (2001) *Indigenous Sex Offender Treatment Program*, Canberra: Australian Institute of Criminology.

Levesque, RJR, (2000) 'Sentencing Sex Crimes Against Children: An Empirical and Policy Analysis' 18(2-3) *Behavioral Sciences and the Law* 331-341.

Lieb, R, (1996) Washington's Sexually Violent Predator Law: Legislative History and Comparisons With Other States, Olympia: Washington State Institute for Public Policy.

Lievore, D, (2004) *Recidivism of Sexual Assault Offenders: Rates, Risk Factors and Treatment Efficacy*, Canberra: Australian Institute of Criminology.

Lievore, D, (2005) 'Thoughts on Recidivism and Rehabilitation of Rapists' 28(1) *University of New South Wales Law Journal* 293-298.

Logan, WA, (1998) 'The Ex Post Facto Clause and the Jurisprudence of Punishment' 35(4) *American Criminal Law Review* 1261-1318.

Macken C, (2005) 'Preventive Detention and the Right of Personal Liberty and Security Under the International Covenant on Civil and Political Rights, 1966' 26 *Adelaide Law Review* 1-28.

Magna Carta (1215).

Maloney, Reeanna, (2008) Prisoners Legal Service, Personal Communication to Professor Keyzer, 11 March 2008.

Management of Offenders etc (Scotland) Act 2005.

Marques, Janice K, Mark Wiedernaders, David M Day, Craig Nelson and Alice van Ommeren, (2005) 'Results from California's Sex Offender Treatment and Evaluation Project (SOTEP)' 17(1) *Sexual Abuse: A Journal of Research and Treatment* 79-107.

McAuley, F, (1993) *Insanity, Psychiatry and Criminal Responsibility,* Dublin: Round Hall Press.

McCallum, D, (2001) *Personality and Dangerousness: Genealogies of Antisocial Personality Disorder,* Cambridge: Cambridge University Press.

McFadyen, N, (2008) 'The Order for Lifelong Restriction: Sentencing for Serious Violent Offenders' <http://www.rmascotland.gov.uk/ViewFile.aspx?id=343>.

McGuire, J, (2008) 'Dilemmas in Correctional Psychology' in G Bourgon, K Hanson, J Pozzulo, K Morton Bourgon and C Tanasichuk (eds) *Proceedings of the 2007 North American Correctional and Criminal Justice Psychology Conference* <http://www.publicsafety.gc.ca/res/cor/rep/2008-02-haccjpc-eng.aspx> 110-117.

McSherry B, (2004) 'Terrorism Offences in the Criminal Code: Broadening the Boundaries of Australian Criminal Laws' 27(2) *University of New South Wales Law Journal* 354-372.

McSherry B, (2005) 'Indefinite and Preventive Detention Legislation: From Caution to an Open Door' 29 *Criminal Law Journal* 94-110.

McSherry, B, (2006) 'Sex, Drugs and Evil Souls: The Growing Reliance on Preventive Detention Regimes' 32(2) *Monash University Law Review* 237-274.

McSherry, B, (2008) 'International Trends in Mental Health Laws' in B McSherry (ed) *International Trends in Mental Health Laws* Sydney: Federation Press.

Melton, G, Petrila, J, Poythress, N and Slobogin, C, (1987) *Psychological Evaluations for the Courts,* New York: Guildford.

Mercado, CC and Ogloff, JRP, (2006) 'Risk and the Preventive Detention of Sex Offenders in Australia and the United States' 20 *International Journal of Law and Psychiatry* 49-59.

Miethe, T, Olson, J and Mitchell, O, (2006) 'Specialisation and Persistence in the Arrest Histories of Sex Offenders – A Comparative Analysis of Alternative Measures and Offense Types' 43(3) *Journal of Research in Crime and Delinquency* 204-229.

Miletich, S, (1989) 'Mother is Upset Over Trust Fund for Mutilated Boy' *Seattle Post-Intelligencer* 28 August 1989 <http://seattlepi.nwsource.com/archives/1989/8901230263.asp>.

Monahan, J, (1981) *The Clinical Prediction of Violent Behavior* National Institute of Mental Health, Washington DC.

Monahan, J, Steadman, HJ, Silver, E, Appelbaum, PS, Robbins, PC, Mulvey, EP, Roth, LH, Grisso, T and Banks, S, (2001) *Rethinking Risk Assessment: The MacArthur Study of Mental Disorder and Violence*, Oxford: Oxford University Press.

Mooney, J, (1992) 'Mutilated Boy's Mother Sues Tacoma Police and Schools' *Seattle Post-Intelligencer* 22 May 1992.

Mooney, J and Holt, G, (1989) 'Clinging to Belief in Innocence – Two Mothers Share a Single Tragedy' *Seattle Post-Intelligencer* 1 June 1989.

Morse, SJ, (2008) 'The Ethics of Forensic Practice: Reclaiming the Wasteland' 36 *The Journal of the American Academy of Psychiatry and the Law* 206-217.

Mullen, PE, (1999) 'Dangerous People with Severe Personality Disorder' 319 *British Medical Journal* 1146-1147.

Mullen, PE, (2001) 'Dangerousness, Risk and the Prediction of Probability' in M Gelder, JJ Lopez-Ibor and N Andresen (eds) *New Oxford Textbook of Psychiatry*, Oxford: Oxford University Press, 2066-2119.

Mullen, PE, (2007) 'Dangerous and Severe Personality Disorder and in Need of Treatment' 190 (suppl 49) *British Journal of Psychiatry ss* 3-7.

Munro O'Brien, J, (2008) 'Chants Disrupt Ferguson Meeting' *The Courier Mail* 8 July 2008.

New Scientist, (2007a) 'Opinion: Sex Offenders: Throwing Away the Key' 21 February 2007.

New Scientist, (2007b) 'Editorial: The Uncomfortable Truth About Sex Crimes' 24 February 2007.

New South Wales Sentencing Council, (2008) *Penalties Relating to Sexual Assault in New South Wales* (Vol 1), August 2008 <http://www.lawlink.nsw.gov.au/sentencingcouncil>.

Norsko, MA and Baranoski, MV, (2005) 'The State of Contemporary Risk Assessment Research' 50(1) *Canadian Journal of Psychiatry* 18-26.

O'Malley, P, (2002) 'Globalizing Risk? Distinguishing Styles of 'neo-liberal' Criminal Justice in Australia and the USA' 2(2) *Criminal Justice* 205-222.

Penalties and Sentences Act 1992 (Qld).

Petrila, J, (2004) 'Emerging Issues in Forensic Mental Health' 75(1) *Psychiatric Quarterly* 3-19.

Pratt, J, (1998) 'The Rise and Fall of Homophobia and Sexual Psychopath Legislation in Postwar Society' 4 *Psychology, Public Policy and Law* 25-49.

Presley, Mari M, (1999) 'Jimmy Ryce Involuntary Civil Commitment for Sexually Violent Predators' Treatment and Care Act: Replacing Criminal Justice with Civil Commitment' 26 *Florida State University Law Review* 487-516.

Prins, H, (1996) 'Risk Assessment and Management in Criminal Justice and Psychiatry' 7(1) *Journal of Forensic Psychiatry* 42-62.

Queensland Correctional Services, (2001) *Queensland Indigenous Sex Offenders Program*. Brisbane: Government Printer.

Queensland Government, (2008) *A New Public Protection Model for the Management of High Risk Sexual Offenders and Violent Offenders* (June 2008) <http://www.correctiveservices.qld.gov.au/Publications/News_and_Events/News/HighRiskoffendersReportJune08.pdf>.

Quinsey, VL, Harris, GT, Rice, ME and Cormier, CA, (1998) *Violent Offenders: Appraising and Managing Risk*. Washington DC: American Psychological Association.

Ra, EP, (2007) 'The Civil Confinement of Sexual Predators: A Delicate Balance' 22(1) *St John's Journal of Legal Commentary* 335-372.

Raffensberger, C and Tickner, J (eds), (1999) *Protecting Public Health and the Environment: Implementing the Precautionary Principle*, Washington DC: Island Press.

Ramsay, P, (2009) 'The Theory of Vulnerable Autonomy and the Legitimacy of Civil Preventative Orders' in B McSherry, A Norrie and S Bronitt (eds) *Regulating Deviance: The Redirection of Criminalisation and the Futures of Criminal Law*, Portland: Hart Publishing, 109-139.

Report of the Committee on Serious Violent and Sexual Offenders, (2000) Scottish Executive, June 2000.

Richardson, L and Freiberg, A, (2004) 'Protecting Dangerous Offenders from the Community' 4(1) *Criminal Justice* 81-102.

Risk Management Authority, (2009a) 'What We Do' <http://www.rmascotland.gov.uk/whatwedo.aspx>.

Risk Management Authority, (2009b) Personal Communication to Professor McSherry Concerning Numbers of Offenders on Orders For Lifelong Restriction, 18 June 2009.

Roberts, L and Indermaur D, (2007) 'Predicting Punitive Attitudes in Australia' 14(1) *Psychiatry, Psychology and Law* 56-65.

Robertson, MD and Walters, G, (2008) 'Many Faces of the Dual-Role Dilemma in Psychiatric Ethics' 42(3) *Australian and New Zealand Journal of Psychiatry* 228-235.

Rose, N, (1998) 'Governing Risky Individuals: The Role of Psychiatry in New Regimes of Control' 5(2) *Psychiatry, Psychology and Law* 177-195.

Rose, N, (2000a) 'Government and Control' 40 *British Journal of Criminology* 321-339.

Rose, N, (2000b) 'Government and Control' in D Garland and R Sparks (eds) *Criminology and Social Theory*, Oxford: Oxford University Press.

Ross, J, (2006) 'US Hiker Dies Four Months After Vicious Attack in Land She Had Loved' *The Scotsman* 2 November 2006 <http://news.scotsman.com/inverness/US-hiker-dies-four-months.2823461.jp>.

Royal College of Psychiatrists, (2005) 'The Psychiatrist, Courts and Sentencing: the Impact of Extended Sentencing on the Ethical Framework of Forensic Psychiatry' 29(2) *Psychiatric Bulletin* 73-77.

Ruschena, D, (2003) 'Determining Dangerousness: Whatever Happened to the Rules of Justice? 10(1) *Psychiatry, Psychology and Law* 122-140.

Salekin, RT, Rogers, R and Sewell, KW, (1996) 'A Review and Meta-analysis of the Psychopathy Checklist and Psychopathy Checklist-Revised: Predictive Validity of Dangerousness' 3 *Clinical Psychology: Science and Practice* 203-215.

Sample, LL and Bray, TM, (2003) 'Predicting Sex Offending from Criminal Offense History' 3 *Criminology and Public Policy* 59-82.

Schweitzer, R and Dwyer, J, (2003) 'Sex Crime Recidivism: Evaluation of a Sexual Offender Treatment Program' 18(11) *Journal of Interpersonal Violence* 1292-1310.

Scottish Executive, (2001) *Serious Violent and Sexual Offenders Criminal Justice* White Paper <http://www.scotland.gov.uk/Resource/Doc/158912/0043171.pdf>.

Scottish Government News Site, (2008) <http://www.scotland.gov.uk/News/News-Today>.

Scottish Parliament, (2001) Debate on Serious Violent and Sexual Offenders <http://www.scottish.parliament.uk/business/officialReports/meetingsParliament/or-01/sor0627-02.htm>.

Seager, JA, Jellicoe, D and Dhaliwal, GK, (2004) 'Refusers, Dropouts and Completers: Measuring Sex Offender Treatment Therapy' (2004) 48(5) *International Journal of Offender Therapy and Comparative Criminology* 600-612.

Seddon, T, (2007) *Punishment and Madness: Governing Prisoners with Mental Health Problems*, Oxford: Routledge-Cavendish.

Seddon, T, (2008) 'Dangerous Liaisons: Personality Disorder and the Politics of Risk' 10(3) *Punishment and Society* 301-317.

Seeman, MV, (2005) 'Psychiatry in the Nazi Era' 50(4) *Canadian Journal of Psychiatry* 218-224.

Sexually Violent Predators Act 1990 (Wash).

Shatzkin, K and Do, A, (1990) 'Shriner Guilty – Jury Convicts Him in Attack on Boy' *The Seattle Times* 7 February 1990.

Simon, J, (1998) 'Managing the Monstrous: Sex Offenders and the New Penology' 4(1/2) *Psychology, Public Policy and Law* 452-467.

Simon, L, (1997) 'Do Criminal Offenders Specialise in Crime Types?' 6(1) *Allied and Preventive Psychology* 35-53.

Slobogin, C, (2006) 'Dangerousness and Expertise Redux' 56(2) *Emory Law Journal* 275-325.

Smith, Douglas, (2008) 'The Constitutionality of Civil Commitment and the Requirement of Adequate Treatment' 49 *Boston College Law Review* 1383-1429.

Special Commitment Center Washington, (2009) 'Employment at the Special Commitment Center' <http://www.dshs.wa.gov/hrsa/scc/Employment.htm>.

Steadman, HJ, (1972-1973) 'The Psychiatrist as a Conservative Agent of Social Control' 20 *Social Problems* 263-270.

Steadman, HJ, (2000) 'From Dangerousness to Risk Assessment of Community Violence: Taking Stock at the Turn of the Century' 28(3) *Journal of the American Academy of Psychiatry and the Law* 265-271.

Stone, AA, (1984) 'The Ethical Boundaries of Forensic Psychiatry: A View from the Ivory Tower' 12 *Bulletin of the American Academy of Psychiatry and Law* 209-219.

Strous, RD, (2007) 'Psychiatry During the Nazi Era: Ethical Lessons for the Modern Professional' 6(8) *Annals of General Psychiatry* (Published online 27 February 2007) <doi:10.1186/1744-859X-6-8>.

STV News, (2009) 'Edinburgh Abuse Case Referred to High Court' 14 April 2009 <http://news.stv.tv/scotland/east-central/ 88287-edinbugrh-abuse-case-referred-to-high-court>.

Sullivan, DH, Mullen PE and Pathé MT, (2005) 'Legislation in Victoria on Sexual Offenders: Issues for Health Professionals' 183(6) *Medical Journal of Australia* 318-320.

Sunstein, CR, (2005) *Laws of Fear: Beyond the Precautionary Principle*, Cambridge: Cambridge University Press.

Sutherland, EH, (1950) 'The Diffusion of Sexual Psychopath Laws' 56 *American Journal of Society* 142-148.

Texas Department of State Health Services, Council on Sex Offender Treatment, (2009) 'Civil Commitment of the Sexually Violent Predator – Costs of Inpatient vs. Outpatient SVP' <http://www.dshs.state.tx.us/csot/csot_ccost.shtm>.

Thampy, K, (2004) Sexual Offences and Human Rights, unpublished LLM thesis, April 2004 <http://www.thampy.com/llmthesis.doc> accessed 13 June 2009.

The Courier-Mail, (1988) 'Child-Sex Offender Jailed for 14 Years' 29 June 1988.

The Courier-Mail, (2009) 'Dennis Ferguson Found Not Guilty of Molesting Girl' 6 March 2009 <http://www.news.com.au/story/0,27574,25146924-421,00.html>.

The Herald, (2009) 'Stalker, 17, Youngest to Receive Lifelong Restriction Order' 12 June 2009 <http://www.theherald.co.uk/news/news/display.var.2442104.0.Stalker_17_youngest_to_receive_lifelong_restriction_order.php>.

The Local, (2007) 'Scot Jailed for Refusing to Pay Massive Restaurant Bill' 7 September 2007 <http://www.thelocal.se/article.php?ID=8427&print=true>.

The Scotsman, (2005) 'Out of Control and a Danger to Women' 23 May 2005 <http://thescotsman.scotsman.com/latestnews/Out-of-control-and-a.2429836.jp>.

The Scotsman, (2008) 'Sex Offender Cronin Jailed for Fraud' 19 January 2008 <http://.news.scotsman.com/scotland/Sex-offender-Cronin-jailed-for.3690899.jp>.

Tuddenham L and Baird J, (2007) 'The Risk Management Authority in Scotland and the Forensic Psychiatrist as Risk Assessor' 31 *Psychiatric Bulletin* 164-166.

United Nations Convention Against Torture and Other Cruel, Inhuman or Degrading Treatment or Punishment (1984) GA Res 39/46; UN DOC A/39/51; 1465 UNTS 85.

United Nations Declaration of Basic Principles of Justice for Victims of Crime and Abuse of Power (1985) GA Res 40/34.

United Nations Standard Minimum Rules for the Treatment of Prisoners (1955) ESC Res 663 C (xxiv) and 2076 (LXII).

Universal Declaration of Human Rights (1948) GA Res 217A(III); UN DOC A/810 at 71.

Walker, N (ed), (1996) *Dangerous People*, Oxford: Blackstone Press.

Ward, T and Eccleston, L, (2000) 'The Assessment of Dangerous Behaviour: Research and Clinical Issues' 17(2) *Behaviour Change* 53-68.

Warner K, (2003) 'Sentencing Review 2002-2003' 27(6) *Criminal Law Journal* 325-340.

Wash Revised Code (1990)-(1995).

Wash Revised Code (1989).

Wash Revised Code Amendments (2009).

Washington Laws (1984).

Washington Revised Code (2002).

Webster, CD, Douglas, KS, Eaves, D, and Hart, SD, (1997) *HCR-20: Assessing Risk for Violence*, version 2, Mental Health, Law, and Policy Institute, Simon Fraser University, Burnaby, British Columbia.

Wettstein, RM (ed), (1992) *Treatment of Offenders with Mental Disorders* New York: Guildford Press.

Willis HR, (2008) 'Creeping by Moonlight: A Look at Civil Commitment Laws for Sexually Violent Predators Through the Lens of the Yellow Wallpaper' 15 *William and Mary Journal of Women and the Law* 161-188.

Wilson, NJ and Wales D, (2008) 'Overview of Treatment: Corrections and Mental Health' in Katarina Fritzon and Paul Wilson (eds) *Forensic Psychology and Criminology an Australian Perspective* 186-201.

Winick, B and La Fond, J (eds), (2003) *Protecting Society from Sexually Dangerous Offenders: Law, Justice and Therapy*, Washington DC: American Psychological Association.

Womersley, T, (2002) '"Walter Mitty Jailed Again"' *The Scotsman* 19 February 2002 <http://news.scotsman.com/latestnews/Walter-Mitty-is-jailed-again.2303705.jp>.

Zedner, L, (2006) 'Neither Safe Nor Sound? The Perils and Possibilities of Risk' 3 *Canadian Journal of Criminology and Criminal Justice* 423-434.

Zedner, L, (2007a) 'Pre-crime and Post-criminology?' 11(2) *Theoretical Criminology* 261-281.

Zedner, L, (2007b) 'Preventive Justice or Pre-Punishment? The Case of Control Orders' 59 *Current Legal Problems* 174-203.

Zedner, L, (2009) 'Fixing the Future?: The Pre-emptive Turn in Criminal Justice' in B McSherry, A Norrie and S Bronitt (eds) *Regulating Deviance: The Redirection of Criminalisation and the Futures of Criminal Law*, Portland: Hart Publishing, 35-58.

Table of Cases

Allen v Illinois 478 US 364 (1986): 51, 57, 58-59, 60, 95
Attorney-General (NSW) v Tillman [2007] NSWSC 605: 30
Attorney-General (Qld) v B [2006] QSC 227: 70, 74, 75, 86
Attorney-General (Qld) v Banks [2007] QSC 267: 70, 74
Attorney-General (Qld) v Beattie [2006] QSC 322: 88
Attorney-General (Qld) v Beattie [2007] QCA 96: 70
Attorney-General (Qld) v Bickle [2006] QSC 130: 75
Attorney-General (Qld) v Bickle [2008] QSC 211: 85
Attorney-General (Qld) v Bragg [2009] QSC 9: 87
Attorney-General (Qld) v Bridson [2007] QSC 307: 70, 73, 75, 88
Attorney-General (Qld) v Bridson [2008] QSC 281: 79
Attorney-General (Qld) v Bryde [2008] QSC 94: 70, 86, 87
Attorney-General (Qld) v Burke [2008] QSC 313: 76
Attorney-General (Qld) v Carpenter [2008] QSC 225: 30, 54, 70, 76
Attorney-General (Qld) v Currie [2009] QSC 112: 71, 76, 89, 93
Attorney-General (Qld) v Deverill [2008] QSC 5: 87, 88
Attorney-General (Qld) v Downs [2005] QSC 16: 86, 89
Attorney-General (Qld) v Downs [2008] QSC 87: 54, 86, 93, 103
Attorney-General (Qld) v Edwards [2007] QSC 396: 75, 89
Attorney-General (Qld) v Fardon [2003] QSC 200: 12
Attorney-General (Qld) v Fardon [2003] QSC 331: 12, 54
Attorney-General (Qld) v Fardon [2003] QCA 416: 12, 107
Attorney-General (Qld) v Fardon [2005] QSC 137: 81, 89
Attorney-General (Qld) v Fardon [2006] QSC 275: 71, 75
Attorney-General (Qld) v Fardon [2006] QCA 512: 74-75, 89-90
Attorney-General (Qld) v Fardon [2007] QSC 299: 89
Attorney-General (Qld) v Fisher [2007] QSC 212: 70
Attorney-General (Qld) v Fisher [2007] QSC 341: 70, 71, 75, 86
Attorney-General (Qld) v Fisher [2009] QSC 104: 87
Attorney-General (Qld) v Foy [2004] QSC 428: 78
Attorney-General (Qld) v Foy [2005] QSC 1: 86, 89
Attorney-General (Qld) v Foy [2007] QSC 141: 75
Attorney-General (Qld) v Francis [2004] QSC 128: 78-79
Attorney-General (Qld) v Francis [2005] QSC 381: 81-82, 90-91
Attorney-General (Qld) v Francis [2006] QCA 324: 53, 54, 75, 85
Attorney-General (Qld) v Francis [2007] QSC 328: 82
Attorney-General (Qld) v Francis [2007] QSC 367: 75, 89
Attorney-General (Qld) v Francis [2007] 1 Qd R 396: 84
Attorney-General (Qld) v Francis [2008] QSC 69: 87, 88
Attorney-General (Qld) v Francis (2008) 250 ALR 555: 87
Attorney-General (Qld) v Friend [2008] QSC 27: 71
Attorney-General (Qld) v Gadd [2008] QSC 247: 11, 30, 78
Attorney-General (Qld) v George [2009] QSC 2: 31, 76, 94
Attorney-General (Qld) v Hancock [2008] QSC 338: 70, 76
Attorney-General (Qld) v Hansen [2006] QSC 35: 75, 89
Attorney-General (Qld) v Harvey [2007] QSC 366: 70

Attorney-General (Qld) v HTR [2007] QSC 19: 75, 89
Attorney-General (Qld) v Hynds [2007] QSC 374: 70, 85, 103
Attorney-General (Qld) v Kondos [2008] QSC 295: 74, 79
Attorney-General (Qld) v Lawrence [2008] QSC 230: 82-84, 103
Attorney-General (Qld) v Lawrence [2009] QCA 136: 84
Attorney-General (Qld) v Levack [2007] QSC 275: 70, 71, 75, 89
Attorney-General (Qld) v Little [2008] QSC 269: 79
Attorney-General (Qld) v LSS [2007] QSC 202: 71, 86, 89
Attorney-General (Qld) v McLean [2006] QSC 137: 30, 31, 72, 74, 75
Attorney-General (Qld) v Murry [2007] QSC 121: 85-86
Attorney-General (Qld) v Nash [2003] QSC 377: 81
Attorney-General (Qld) v Nash (2003) 143 A Crim R 312: 55, 69, 78
Attorney-General (Qld) v Oliver [2009] QSC 34: 100
Attorney-General (Qld) v O'Rourke [2006] QSC 196: 75
Attorney-General (Qld) v O'Rourke [2008] QSC 153: 87, 88
Attorney-General (Qld) v Pearce [2005] QSC 314: 44
Attorney-General (Qld) v Perkins [2009] QSC 53: 73, 88
Attorney-General (Qld) v Reynolds [2007] QSC 52: 89
Attorney-General (Qld) v Robinson [2006] QSC 328: 71
Attorney-General (Qld) v Robinson [2007] QCA 111: 71, 75, 89, 91-92
Attorney-General (Qld) v Sambo [2008] QSC 262: 76, 84-85, 87
Attorney-General (Qld) v Shapland [2007] QSC 344: 70, 71
Attorney-General (Qld) v Smith [2008] QSC 22: 75
Attorney-General (Qld) v Sutherland [2006] QSC 268: 74, 75
Attorney-General (Qld) v Taylor [2008] QSC 183: 54, 85, 100
Attorney-General (Qld) v Toms [2006] QSC 298: 76, 77
Attorney-General (Qld) v Toms [2007] QSC 290: 89, 93
Attorney-General (Qld) v Toms [2008] QSC 131: 87, 93
Attorney-General (Qld) v Thumm [2008] QSC 180: 87
Attorney-General (Qld) v Twigge [2006] QSC 107: 71, 72, 76, 88
Attorney-General (Qld) v Van Dessel [2006] QSC 16: 44, 54, 69-70, 76
Attorney-General (Qld) v Van Dessel [2006] QCA 285: 71
Attorney-General (Qld) v Voois [2008] QSC 168: 70, 88
Attorney-General (Qld) v W [2004] QSC 262: 72, 79, 85
Attorney-General (Qld) v Waghorn [2006] QSC 171: 54, 70, 85
Attorney-General (Qld) v Watego [2003] QSC 367: 76
Attorney-General (Qld) v Watego (2003) 142 A Crim R 537: 55, 69, 78
Attorney-General (Qld) v Wilson [2009] QSC 36: 76, 87
Attorney-General (Qld) v Winston [2009] QSC 11: 70, 86
Attorney-General (Qld) v Wright [2006] QSC 389: 71
Attorney-General (Qld) v Wright [2008] QSC 237: 87
Attorney-General (Qld) v WW [2007] QCA 334: 70
Attorney-General (Qld) v Yeo [2006] QSC 63: 70, 76
Attorney-General (Qld) v Yeo [2007] QSC 274: 70, 89
Attorney-General (Qld) v Yeo [2008] QCA 115: 70, 85
Chu Kheng Lim v Minister for Immigration (1992) 176 CLR 1: 42, 76
Coco v The Queen (1994) 179 CLR 427: 54
Cronin v Her Majesty's Advocate [1993] SCCR 158: 13-14
Director of Public Prosecutions v Ferguson [2003] QSC 1: 7
Director of Public Prosecutions (WA) v Mangolamara [2007] WASC 71: 31
Fardon v Attorney-General (Qld) (2004) 223 CLR 575: 12, 44, 45-46, 49-50, 52, 55-56, 87, 105
Fardon v Attorney-General (Qld) [2006] QSC 5: 79
Ferguson v The Queen [2009] HCA Trans 16: 9

Ferguson v Watterson [2008] QDC 224: 6, 8
Francis *see* Attorney-General (Qld) v Francis
Gough v Southern Queensland Regional Parole Board [2008] QSC 222: 72-73, 75
Illinois v Allen 481 NE 2d 690 (1985): 57
Kable v Director of Public Prosecutions (1995) 36 NSWLR 374: 43
Kable v Director of Public Prosecutions (NSW) (1996) 189 CLR 51: 45
Kansas v Crane 534 US 407 (2002): 6, 60
Kansas v Hendricks 521 US 346 (1997): 6, 50, 51, 57, 59-60
Malloy v Hogan 378 US 1 (1964): 57-58
Polyukhovich v Commonwealth (1991) 172 CLR 501: 52
Power v The Queen (1974) 131 CLR 623: 46
R v Ferguson [2008] QDC 136: 9
R v Ferguson; Ex parte Attorney-General (Qld) [2008] QCA 227: 9
Rameka v New Zealand No 1090/2002 [2003] UNHRC 62 (15 December 2003): 48, 49, 50, 51, 79
RJE v Secretary to the Department of Justice [2008] VSCA 265: 30
Seling v Young 531 US 250 (2001): 6, 57, 60, 96, 106
Shriner v Rohlings et al Civil Action No 07-3306-SAC, 13 February 2008: 6
Turay v Richards No C91-0664RSM, 2007 WL 983132: 95
Turay v Weston No C91-664WD (WD Wash 1994): 97
Veen v The Queen (No 1) (1979) 143 CLR 458: 41
Veen v The Queen (No 2) (1988) 164 CLR 465: 41
Williams v The Queen (1986) 161 CLR 278: 54
Young v Weston 898 F Supp 744 (WD Wash 1995): 6
Young, Re Personal Restraint of, 857 P 2d 989 (Wash 1993): 6

Index

Actuarial justice, 20
Anti-social behaviour orders, 21
Arbitrary detention, 47-48, 49, 67
Australian Human Rights Commission, 45, 46, 47
Bill of Rights
Australia, 44
United States of America, 56, 105, 106
Community groups, outcry against sex offenders by, 1, 19, 104
Community notification powers, 3, 97
Community protection, 1, 10, 87, 111
balance of individual rights with, 18
detention of sex offenders and, 42, 103
medical model of treatment rather than criminal justice model and, 33
Continuing detention orders, 12, 54, 79, 80-81, 83
Criminal justice policy
circuits of inclusion and exclusion and, 22
sectoral shift by state and, 21-22
shift to pre-crime society and, 20-21
Cronin, John, 1, 12-17, 104
'Dangerousness', 19, 20, 27, 33, 42, 49, 50
Detention of sex offenders *see* **Preventive detention and supervision schemes**
Double jeopardy, 50, 60, 105
European Convention on Human Rights, 66, 105, 106, 113
Fardon, Robert John, 11-12, 44, 45-46, 47, 48, 49-50, 52, 54, 55-56, 71, 74-75, 79, 81, 87, 89-90, 105, 107
Ferguson, Dennis, 1, 6-12, 23, 104
Forensic psychiatry, 32, 33
Forensic psychology, 32, 76
Future harm, prevention of, 19, 107
coercive measures and, 20
'precautionary principle' and, 22
'radical prevention' and, 21
risk assessment orders and, 26
Historical/Clinical/Risk-20 (HCR-20) scale, 27
Human rights
preventive detention and supervision schemes and, 40, 43, 44, 104, 105-107
Indefinite sentencing, 41, 105
'determinate plus sentencing', 109
reluctance of Australian courts to use, 110
International Covenant on Civil and Political Rights, 43, 53, 105
Article 9, 48, 49
Article 9(1), 47
Article 14(7), 47, 48, 49
Article 15(1), 52
First Optional Protocol, 47
'Iterative' classification tree (ICT) scale, 27
'Justice ethics', 35-36
Kane, Gene Raymond, 3
Law reform, 18
continuing detention of sex offenders and, 42
Less Restrictive Alternatives, 96
Liberty, deprivation of, 21, 33, 36, 37, 42-43, 59, 80, 100, 101
Liberty principle, 53-54
Media, outcry against sex offenders by, 1-2, 17, 104
'Mental abnormality, 5, 18, 26, 59, 61, 62, 108
Mental health laws, inclusion of sex offenders in, 4, 62-63

Mental health professionals, as agents of social control, 36, 37, 38
Mental health professionals, assessment of risk by, 20, 25-32, 77, 108
cautious nature of, 27
'dangerousness' and, 27
for purpose of detention on imprisonment, 20
scale based approach, 27
tension amongst, 31-32
Mental health professionals, giving of evidence by, 32-37, 108
always ethical, 34-35
always unethical, 33-34
ethical except for post-sentence preventive detention schemes, 36-37
ethical in certain circumstances, 35-36
respect for persons and, 36
Offenders
'dangerous', criminal justice systems and, 19
high risk, 1
indefinite sentencing and, 41
procedural fairness and, 54-56
Indigenous, 31
registers of, 3, 21
rights of, 1, 18, 42, 43, 53
risk assessment of *see* Risk assessment
sex *see* Sex offenders
Orders for lifelong restriction (OLRs), 99-102
Paedophiles
as archetypal sex offenders, 23
community concerns about, 10
definition, 61
Periodic review, 49, 52, 55, 79
'Personality disorder', 5, 13, 108
'Precautionary principle', 22, 38
Predictive testimony, 36
Preventive detention and supervision schemes, 1, 104
as form of social control, 61, 62, 108
curtailment of liberty and, 21, 37, 43, 53-54
elimination of sexual offending and, 40-41
'false positives' and, 31, 108
human rights principles and, 40, 43, 44, 104, 105-107
political popularity of, 20
New South Wales, 12, 44, 46, 51, 105, 112
politics of fear and insecurity and, 23
post-sentence, 41-42, 48-49, 51-52, 105, 110
constitutional validity of, 56-57
Queensland *see* **Queensland model**
rise of, 18, 38
risk assessment and *see* **Risk assessment**
Scotland *see* **Scotland model**
sentencing reform and, 108-110
success in reducing reoffending rates and, 1, 18, 40, 71-72, 77
treatment and, 35, 60, 62, 70-76
Western Australia, 12, 44, 46, 51, 112
Washington State *see* **Washington State model**
Principle of procedural fairness, 54-56, 69, 81, 101
Principle of proportionality, 41-42, 105
finality of sentence and, 51-52
Principle of retrospectivity, 52-53
Privilege against self-incrimination, 57
Psychiatrists, 25, 26
as risk assessors, 32, 76, 108
forensic, 38
evidence of, 35, 37
prediction of dangerousness and, 33
Psychologists, 25, 26
as risk assessors, 32, 76, 108
forensic, 39, 77
prediction of dangerousness and, 33
Psychopathy Check-List Revised (PCL-R), 27-28
Queensland Corrective Services, 11, 68, 73, 74, 102

employment of psychologists by, 76-77
implementation of treatment plans and, 81-83, 86, 88
post release accommodation and services and, 88, 93-94
Wacol Prison Reserve, 93, 94, 111
proposal to lengthen continuing detention orders, 80
Sexual Offender Dangerous Offender Unit, 83
Queensland model, 1, 10-11, 18
cognitive impairment of prisoners and, 86
Dangerous Prisoners (Sexual Offenders) Act 2003, 10-11, 25, 42, 45-46, 49, 51, 56, 112
annual reviews and, 79-81
applications under, 78-79
breach of supervision orders under, 87
constitutional validity of, 12, 18, 44-45, 105
introduction and passing of, 68
liberty principle and, 53-54
popular demand for retributive treatment and, 47
procedural fairness and, 54-56, 81
requirement to protect human rights and, 44
retrospective operation of, 52-53, 105
risk assessment process of, 76-77
strain on administrative departments and, 68-69, 110
supervision orders under, 85-86, 106
treatment issues and, 70-76, 79, 80, 81-85, 102-103
trends in case law related to, 70-71
detention in prison and double punishment and, 44-51, 71, 105
human rights principles and, 40, 44, 105-106, 114
implementation issues, 68-94
independent system of risk assessment in, 77
liberty principle and, 53-54
'mental abnormality' and, 18
evidence by mental health professionals and, 37
reduction in reoffending and, 71-72, 77
rehabilitation of sexual offenders and, 10, 11, 53, 69, 73, 75
policy setting of, 43-56
post-release accommodation and services and, 88-94, 111-112
Serious Sexual Offenders Review Committee, 11, 78, 81
serious sexual offence, definition of, 11
Sexual Offender Maintenance Program, 88
substance abuse by offenders and, 75-76, 87
'Radical prevention', 21
Reoffending, 24, 70, 71, 72, 89, 108, 109, 111
Retroactive laws, prevention against, 52-53
Risk and precaution, politics of, 18, 19-39, 104
current criminal policy and, 20-22
main themes of, 20
statistical forms of inference and, 27
see also **Mental health professionals, risk assessment**
Risk assessment, 15-16, 17, 64, 107-108
actuarial and clinical assessment of, 31, 37
actuarial risk assessment scales and, 27, 37, 76, 108
application of group data to individuals by, 30
courtroom use of predictions for treatment in, 31-32
criticisms of, 29-32
differences in groups and, 31
issues dealt with in, 28
static/historical variables and, 29-30
as evidence, 32-33